Dynamic
Duos

Dynamic Duos

THE ALPHA/BETA KEY
TO UNLOCKING SUCCESS
IN GAY RELATIONSHIPS

Keith W. Swain
Psy.D.

alyson books
NEW YORK

© 2008 by Keith W. Swain

Manufactured in the United States of America

This trade paperback original is published by Alyson Books
245 West 17th Street, New York, NY 10011

Distribution in the United Kingdom by Turnaround Publisher Services Ltd.
Unit 3, Olympia Trading Estate, Coburg Road, Wood Green
London N22 6TZ England

First Edition: July 2008

08 09 10 11 12 13 14 15 16 17 a 10 9 8 7 6 5 4 3 2 1

ISBN-10 1-559350-067-X
ISBN-13 978-1-59350-067-2

Library of Congress Cataloging-in-Publication data are on file.

Cover design by Victor Mingovits

To Thomas, for "Once upon a time..."

and

To Dennis, for "Happily ever after..."

Contents

Acknowledgments

While the myth is that all writers write alone, nothing written, at least that ends up in print, is the result of a single person. Behind each printed word stands a family of people dedicated to creating the best reading experience possible. This book is no different. With that in mind, I want to thank those people who have been a part of my creative family.

Publishing a book is a winding path from start to finish. At the beginning, there are your friends. Lauren Sinclair and Bob Dubac were supportive from the start. To Davol Tedder, Lane Jones, Ann Bersani, David Ford, Craig Oliver, Michael Richters, Carlos Cobos, and David Comeau, your willingness to read and comment was touching at the time and greatly appreciated now. I am also grateful for those professionals who offered me help, guidance, and respect early in the process, especially editor and teacher Alice Levine and fellow writer Mark Obmascik. And just like everyone in publishing tells you (even though you don't want to believe them), it takes an agent to sell a book. Luckily for me, I have the support and determined effort of two: Jeffery McGraw and Cricket Freeman of the August Agency. Thanks especially to Jeffery for your almost daily support and guidance.

I wish I were such a brilliant writer that I could write perfectly, but I'm not. Instead, I've had great editors who have helped me throughout my career. I'd like to thank Barbara Ellis and Greg Moore at the *Denver Post*, Jonathan Wolman of the *Detroit News*, and Greg Montoya at *Out Front Colorado*. My history with good editors continued with this book. I'd like to thank Joseph Pittman for supporting this book from the start, and Linda Carbone for shepherding it through the editorial development process.

The research that formed the basis of this book, the National Male Relationship Survey, would have been impossible without the support of Tim Gill and the men of Connexion.org. I would also like to thank two incredible women who can do what I can't—think mathematically—for their computing advice and statistical analysis. Without the help of Denise Wallace and Monica Geist, I would still be stuck in *Excel for Dummies*. I also want to thank Marcia Swain for her unending support and legal advice and Nolan Epple for his calm sanity and ongoing friendship. And of course, every gay guy needs a straight guy to translate the real world for him. My thanks to Michael Durkin for being my conduit to the other side.

The majority of this book was written in the warm comfort of the Metropolis coffee shop in Denver. Thanks to Brock Wortman for not charging me rent. And it goes without saying that without the constant supply of caffeine supplied by Meagan, Chris, Chelsea, and Nick, this book would have never been finished. Now if I could just get my hands to stop shaking...

Finally, I am grateful to my family. In the chaos of daily life, my partner, Dennis, and our son, Thomas, have happily offered me peace and quiet when I needed to disappear and write. And of course, I'd be remiss if I didn't acknowledge my constant writing companion, Auggie, our loving Golden Retriever, who even now sleeps at my feet.

The Path to Long-Term Relationships

Superhero in Search of Sidekick. I tend to be a loner, but don't want to be anymore.

—personal ad, *In Touch* magazine

RIGHT NOW. No one ever says "later." They always say "right now." Whenever I ask my patients, or friends, or the men who attend my relationship workshops when they want to meet the perfect man, they always say, "Right now." I certainly remember that feeling. When we need something as badly as we need love, there's never any desire to wait. The question I always have is, Why *do* so many wait?

Two years ago, I remember waking up one morning and looking across at my partner, sleeping, and thinking to myself, "Good God, he's still here." It makes me laugh writing this now—it sounds as if I wished he were gone. What I meant, of course, was that I couldn't believe that after more than twenty years together, he'd still be willing to put up with me.

I have worked as a gay couples counselor for almost my entire adult life, over twenty-five years now. Over those years, I have met literally hundreds of gay couples and single men trying to find love, approaching love the same way one would explore the caves of Endor: too often diving in without a map, unsure of what to look for, and equipped with little more than a flashlight and dreams of treasure. "Hello, anyone in here?"

That morning, I remember thinking to myself, "I'm lucky."

But as a social scientist, I knew better. Love is not a matter of luck. It's a matter of confidence and intention.

At least it is for heterosexual men and women. They come out of their adolescent years confident that they will find someone and fully intent on doing just that. And an amazing number of them succeed. By the age of forty-five, 75 percent of heterosexual men are married or have a live-in partner. The average gay man at that age, on the other hand, will have had two significant relationships that have ended, generally unhappily. Why? What is it about gay guys that makes it so hard to find and keep lifelong love? Let's face it: something isn't working.

Though I was happily married to my partner, most of my clients haven't been either happy or happily married. It's in my nature to want people to be happy, and I want to provide them with good, working answers to their problem. To provide those answers, I started my own personal quest. I dove into everything I could get my hands on about gay male relationships, determined to find out what was keeping so many gay men on the outside, peering through the chapel windows, instead of walking down the aisle.

What I found was disappointing: a mélange of how-to books, personal counselors, relationship experts, and dating Web sites—all giving advice based on hearsay, anecdotes, and weak assumptions about human behavior. And I heard from my clients, who had tried them all, that these "answers" didn't work. As one of my clients told me, that if-you-visualize-him-he'll-come crap wasn't cutting it. Not for my clients, nor for me. There had to be a better approach. Thus, *Dynamic Duos* was born.

As the title of this book implies, and as you'll see in the thematic thread throughout this book, gay men, while we may not be superheroes, do have an awful lot in common with them. We tend to be outsiders, we see things from a different angle, and we are men who, too often, are harshly aware of the injustices of the world. And most markedly, we also prefer the company of men to women. In fact, we *love* the company of men, yet nothing seems to confuse us more. We're amazingly good at exploring the farthest reaches of the sexual universe, yet we're terrible at marriage. We are so bad at relationships that we mention our breakups as if they were simply a change in the weather. "How's Jim?" "Jim? Oh, we broke up…" Tears? Rarely. More likely a slight grin, a "you-know-how-it-goes" smirk. That's not to be critical. It just seems to be our nature.

Love is by far the most common natural experience of every human being. Even if we have a hard time managing love, there's no denying that we gay men certainly desire it. Thus began the two-year journey into the nature of love and relationships that became this book—a journey that brought wonderful new insights and, yes, finally, *science-based* answers for gay men on how to find, and keep, love.

Not surprisingly, this path wasn't a superhighway—more like the plotline of a DC Comic, with plenty of twists and turns along the way. And as in any good superhero adventure, this journey required a suspension of assumptions and a mind open to new ideas, ideas that have been challenging to me and, at times, will be to you. Almost everything that you have read and known about gay men, gay relationships, and maybe even yourself may come into question in the following pages.

Yet, unlike those gay men wandering lost in the caves of love, I'm going to offer you a map: this book, handily divided into a series of parts, which are, in turn, divided into chapters, all designed to bring you, step by step, to the same amazing realization that I have come to: long-term gay relationships are not only possible for every gay man but probable, if we understand the true *nature* of gay male relationships.

Nature is the underlying answer, of course. In the debate over whether homosexuality results from nature or nurture, nature has taken a strong lead. What has been lagging behind in this race, though, is our understanding of how nature also directs matters of the heart. *Dynamic Duos* intends to rectify that.

In Part I, we begin by examining the unsettling truth about the nature of gay male relationships today. Though a majority of gay men claim to want a lifelong love, few find it. At any given time, less than 13 percent of the American gay male population is in a relationship—in fact, the majority of gay men tend to spend more time alone than with someone. Even with the divorce rate in the United States approaching 50 percent, straight men are still far more successful—over three times more successful—than most gay men in finding and keeping love in their lives. Why? This uncomfortable truth is just the tip of a melting relationship iceberg. But not to worry—like all good hero stories, there's good news on the horizon.

What are heterosexual men and women doing that we aren't? As I started exploring this subject, I wondered whether there were clues to be found in their love lives. In Part II, we dive into the most basic, evolutionary aspects of human mating, seeking any clue to what may be blocking success for gay men. After all, humans are evolutionarily designed to love and live in pairs. Why not gay men? Heterosexual marriages tend to work at least half the time. Lesbian relationships tend to be successful around 70 percent of the time. Yet gay relationships tend to *fail*—succeeding less than 20 percent of the time. We have to ask the obvious question: "What do the first two types of relationships have that gay relationships don't?" The answer is Clue No. 1: women.

The next step, of course, would be to look deeper into the current scientific research into homosexuality. While gay relationships are rarely the focus of scientific research, the biology of homosexuality in general has come into its own over the last decade. Much of the research in this field has been focused on specific "gay traits." Here's a good example. One researcher found that a majority of gay men have fingerprint patterns similar to the fingerprints of women. Interesting, yes, but in my mind, it begs the question, Why does this trait show up only in a *majority* of gay men tested, not in *all* gay men tested? I couldn't help but wonder about the back stories of these other men. If they were gay, why didn't they have the "gay trait"? Aha! Clue No. 2. Is it possible that gay men come in two different *biological* types—say, an Alpha version and a Beta version? And could such a difference play a role in successful relationships?

In Part III, we attempt to get a clearer picture of just that. How? By asking a group of gay men, both single and in couples, about a variety of aspects of their love lives. Over two thousand of my now closest friends responded, and in their answers we found answers—and the final clue to the Alpha/Beta Key to success in long-term gay relationships.

In Part IV, we put our newfound knowledge to work, showing you how to use the Alpha/Beta Key to unlock success in your own dynamic duo. Finally, we look at the effect of life stages on relationships, dating, and marriage in Part V.

Love isn't magic—it just feels that way. There is no other feeling as great as being in love: that excitement that comes from a first returned call, a whispered secret in the dark after twenty years together, or a gentle kiss from an unexpected source. Such dynamic love—a love marked by an unusually continuous and productive experience of contentment and growth—makes us feel like superheroes, as if we are suddenly powerful enough not only to leap tall buildings in a single bound, but also to defeat our evil nemesis, loneliness, which we know lurks on the far side.

That has certainly been my life experience. No one should unwillingly live life alone, when there is a way not to. I wear a gold band inscribed inside with my wedding vow: *Haud diutius unus; meus diligo usquequaque,* "No longer alone; my love always." I am confident that by the end of this book, you, too, will be prepared to live in a dynamic duo of your own.

Part I

IN WHICH WE LEARN
WHAT THE PROBLEM IS

As our story begins, we find a world filled with darkness, our hero, alone, floundering in isolation, unsettled by the growing darkness of an uncomfortable world.

CHAPTER 1

Superman in Plain Clothes: The Search for Lifelong Love

In the era of the heroic Guardians of the Galaxy, our hero, Batwing, was one of a dozen Havenites who ruled the planet Haven. Batwing was devastated when his gay partner, Rhodney, was killed by Charlie-27 of the Guardians while defending Batwing. After Haven was destroyed by the Phoenix-Force, Batwing and the rest of Rancor's forces vow to seek vengeance against the Guardians of the Galaxy.

—Gayleague.com

UNLIKE BATWING, vengeance isn't our goal—love is. Wouldn't it be great if we could just snap our fingers or call out some secret word like Captain Marvel's "shazam!" and meet the love of our lives? I know one of my greatest frustrations when I was first coming to terms with my sexuality was how *easy* it seemed for straight men and women to meet. For goodness' sake, they could just walk up to *anyone* they found attractive and ask for a date. And even back then, I realized that there were millions of them and only a few of us.

Since then, though, I've grown a bit more sympathetic to the mating problems that keep some heterosexuals single. But the system really is set up to work for them—for us, not so much. And it shows. If we compare heterosexual marriages to homosexual long-term relationships according to the same criteria, we're not very good at it.

While I have personally known many male couples, through my practice and my daily life, who have made and kept commitments to each other for a lifetime, I'd be dishonest if I said long-term success was the norm, especially if I did so just to be polite. The truth is that a successful, *lifelong* relationship between two men is the exception, because we're not very good at maintaining lifelong relationships.

Here are some numbers to think about. For heterosexual men, at any given time in adult life, over 75 percent are married; by the age of fifty-five, 96 percent of heterosexual men are (or have been) married. According to 2000 U.S. Census data, heterosexual marriages last an average of 24.5 years, with the majority ending with the death of a spouse, not with divorce.

For most gay men, on the other hand, the outlook for lifelong love isn't so rosy. Using information from the 2006 National Survey of Male Relationships, the 1995 Partners National Survey of Lesbian & Gay Couples, and the 2000 U.S. Census, we know that approximately 13 percent of gay men are in relationships at any given time. We further note that the average life span of a gay relationship is only five years. To make matters even gloomier, it appears that most gay men spend more time being single than being partnered. In other words, the time between relationships tends to be longer than the time spent in those relationships.

Of course, the prognosis is gloomy only if we assume that gay men want long-term relationships. I suppose it's possible that gay men prefer to go through life in a series of short-term relationships, as opposed to one for the long run. But the evidence doesn't seem to support that assumption. For example, two of the online gay matching sites, Match.com and Gay.com, claim over a million subscribers seeking, in their terminology, long-term relationships. In addition, many surveys conducted over the last decade indicate that seeking a life partner is the No. 1 concern of gay men. I can certainly say that wanting a life partner but being unable to find one is the No. 1 complaint I hear from my clients. It also seems to be the No. 1 complaint I hear from my gay friends, and the friends of gay men I know, and the friends of friends of single gay men I know. In other words, if gay men really don't want to be married, they sure seem to act or at least talk as if they do.

But perhaps comparing gay relationships to heterosexual marriages is comparing apples to oranges. Maybe gay men really are happier and more contented in short-term connections? Unlikely. In responses to the National Survey of Male Relationships (NSMR) , an online survey of over two thousand gay men I conducted in 2006, gay men in relationships longer than ten years rated their marriages the happiest—slightly higher, in fact, than happiness levels of comparable hetero-sexual marriages. Gay men in short-term relationships, though, tended not to rate those relationships as highly.

Ironically, as the desire for a long-term relationship grows, there also seems to be a growing sense of pessimism among gay men when it comes to the possibility of finding lifelong love. No matter what others may say, let me assure you there are magical, loving, powerful, lifelong relationships out there for gay men, especially for those men who believe in love, a key component to success.

Again, according to the National Survey of Male Relation-ships, 53 percent of the total respondents believed in love at first sight. Here's an interesting detail from that survey question: of those men who had been in relationships longer than ten years and who rated their partnership as "highly gratifying," 100 percent of them not only said they believed in love at first sight, they also said that was how their relationships had begun!

Desire and gas stations may seem to be an odd combination, but for me, they are intimately tied together. I grew up around gas stations, as my dad owned a series of them across the South. I knew early the amazing eroticism that blue-collar men could carry. These were workingmen who wore their sweat as a badge of pride, who scrubbed their dirty nails with Lava soap and wore Old Spice on weekends.

I spent many an hour hanging out in the garage bays, pretending to be interested in car motors, only to smell their manly scent and to perhaps brush against these grease monkey gods.

One time there was a guy I fell for immediately—I would have married him in a minute. That first day we made eye contact, we "accidentally" met in the employee restroom. Within minutes of him showing me his hard-on, I was blowing him, sweat running down his legs and my face and back, the humidity of that small, locked bathroom rising by the minute.

While the encounter was solely sexual on his part, in my dreams I would have married him. I imagined setting up house, being held by him while I slept, protected from

IS A LIFELONG GAY RELATIONSHIP, A MARRIAGE, WHAT YOU'RE LOOKING FOR?

Over my lifetime, I have seen the terminology for gay love move through a variety of phases: from "friend" to "special friend" to "roommate" to "lover" to "significant other" to "partner" to "husband." Though many feel that this is simply semantics, there is a connection between these words and how we (and others) the dangers of the world. I can remember all too well what happened to him. After our one afternoon quickie, he couldn't get away from me fast enough, making sure to call me faggot in front of the other mechanics as he left that day.

Such encounters were the beginning of a greater frustration of my gay life: meeting men and having sex in hopes of establishing a greater connection, a relationship, only to discover that, for many men, sex was both the beginning and the end of any connection. Between men and women, sex is often an unconscious agreement of exchange: women give sex in exchange for emotional connection with men. Sadly, in most gay sexual encounters I've had, there was a built-in masculine conflict: my desire for an emotional connection competing against my other self, a desire for a good fuck. For too many of us, this conflict plays out in confusing sexual/dating encounters. Too often, we assume good sex means good marriage potential or that a bad sexual encounter means a bad potential long-term partner. But it doesn't seem to keep me from falling in love ten times a day.

—Jon, 51

feel and react. Here's a classic example: love and marriage. Though many people intertwine these two words, a marriage moves well beyond love. But what is love, really? Here's a practical social-scientific definition of a love relationship from the psychologist Robert Sternberg, one that works for both heterosexual couples and gay men, and one we'll base our discussion on: "Love is a combination of emotions, thoughts, and behaviors that result from an intimate relationship, with a relationship being understood as an association in which two people influence each other's lives and engage jointly in the many activities of daily life."

According to Sternberg, a healthy love relationship encompasses three key components: passion, commitment, and intimacy. Ideal relationships, those that survive and thrive, are balanced and strongly focused on these three elements and become what Sternberg called consummate love.

Too often, for a variety of reasons, gay men find themselves in some variation of consummate love, lacking one or more of the essential components. Often, initial passion is considered enough for a long-term marriage, a common mistake made by men new to coming out. But such passion alone is simply infatuation, not consummate love. This book is dedicated to helping you find all three components of consummate love: passion, intimacy, and above all, commitment—in other words, a marriage.

Throughout this book, you will see that I move freely between the terms "marriage" and "relationship," though honestly I feel the term "relationship" is so nebulous that it has little value. In fact, it may be damaging to our long-term goal of finding a lifelong love. We have a deep understanding of the social and legal implications of the terms "marriage" and "divorce." If I asked you what the term was for ending a relationship, you may have a harder time coming up with one than if I asked the same question about a marriage. You probably would say "a breakup," yet to me, "breakup" doesn't have half the emotional power that "divorce" has. The problem with using the term "marriage," of course, is the legal aspect—which, of course, rarely applies to gay relationships these days. Nonetheless I'll use the word as often as I can, as I feel it reflects more closely what we mean when we say "lifelong love" or "long-term gay relationship."

So with that said, do you really want to be married?

We get our first hint that superhero Apollo might be gay after he collapses in a battle with the forces of Sliding Albion, as Midnighter, Apollo's partner in fighting evil, cradles Apollo close to his chest as if it might be their last moment together. Later, in issue #28, Seth attacks Midnighter. The Engineer saves Midnighter's life in the next issue. By the end of the story, Apollo and Midnighter celebrate their love with a commitment ceremony.

—GayLeague.com

DO YOU REALLY WANT TO BE MARRIED?

I usually get an odd look when I ask my clients this question. But I'm quite serious. Few gay men I know really comprehend what it means to get married. (I'll give you that few straight men do, either. Women seem better equipped to deal with the concepts involved in a long-term relationship.) Perhaps it's a stereotype, but in our society there has always been the idea that men, by their nature, are hesitant to marry, whereas women are far more likely to want to be married. And as we have seen, gay men tend to form relationships that last an average of just five years. If that works for you, then great—but we're seeking answers to questions about long-term relationships, those that last a lifetime.

There may be some evolutionary basis for men forming relatively short-term relationships. The evolutionary design for the male role in reproduction creates a need for men to find many, and many different, sex partners; it helps diversify the gene pool. This could be the basis for the stereotype that men don't want to "settle down" with one woman. As gay men, do we desire a permanent relationship, or are we driven by an organic need to find multiple sex partners? In heterosexual men, this drive has been managed by the mating desires of women. In gay male relationships, is there some similar managing force? In some relationships, yes; in others, no. The ones using some form of management tend to last, to become what I would call a marriage.

Marriage is a *total life commitment* of two men to each other. You can't be sort of married. A married couple agrees to a lifetime of taking care of each other, through "good times and bad, for better or worse," as the ceremony goes. For many men, the only hesitation may be limiting oneself to sex with only one man. For others, the concern may be bigger, a concern of being limited in all matters of romance and living arrangements. But for all of these concerns there are answers.

Do you want a lifelong connection with another person, in which not only are you taken care of when you're in need, but you also take on full responsibility for your partner when he needs you? In exchange for accepting these responsibilities, you are rewarded with safety, security, and contentment. The ultimate question you will have to answer, both to yourself and to your life partner, is, "Are you willing to take on the responsibilities that marriage brings in exchange for the benefits?"

For many gay couples, an "escape clause" has been too readily available and too hastily used. The biggest challenge for gay men as individuals is not *finding* men to love, but *maintaining* that love. The ultimate secret to long-term marriage is this: you must find love for your partner's human frailties as well as for those attributes that are easy to love. Loving his weaknesses is the ultimate challenge, but one that, when accomplished, is beyond rewarding. It is the greatest example of being able to move beyond self. This is the greatest expression of love.

For those of you who are unsure whether you want a long-term relationship, let me remind you that the need to care for

Derek was the sexiest, cutest, most athletic boy in high school. I wasn't. But somehow we connected. He liked me, and I liked him. Actually, I loved him. I'm not sure how we became best friends, but at some point, we had. What Derek saw in me, I am unsure. I do know that being my friend wasn't the easiest thing. I was the class geek, the school fag, carrot top, string bean, zit face.

We'd camp out and get drunk on Boone's Farm strawberry wine. On long weekends, we'd take my father's car and hit the road for an impromptu trip. I'd let him drive. Just sitting next to Derek was to be in his spotlight. In his friendship, I found a sense of acceptance.

In our senior year, the three of us—Derek, Sharon (Derek's girlfriend), and I—started a unique ritual, getting a room at the Motel 6 every Friday night. Derek said soldiers from the nearby military base often would rent rooms there by the hour, so three high-schoolers renting a room without luggage didn't seem to faze the desk clerk. Sharon and I would wait in the car while Derek went in to rent the room. To save money, he'd always ask for a room with a single bed.

After we had settled in, Derek would produce a bottle of dark rum he'd pilfered from his folk's liquor cabinet, and I'd play bartender, mixing rum and Cokes for the three of us. We'd drink, watch TV, and sometimes Sharon and Derek would make out. They never went further, at least while I was there. After a few hours, Derek would take Sharon home while I waited back at the motel. He'd return and the two of us would get into the single bed to spend the night. He'd sleep in his briefs sometimes. At other times he'd sleep naked. I always wore my shorts, even though I don't think they ever hid my obvious erection.

After we'd turn the lights out, I'd lay there on my back, listening for Derek's breathing to become deeper and more rhythmic, a sign that he was asleep. Once he was asleep, I'd begin what was surely the most nerve-racking, yet for me, an almost necessary ritual. I loved him so much, I was so drawn to him, that I'd lie there in the dark, my heart aching at the same time my cock would be straining against my shorts. And he'd lie there, half covered by a sheet, his naked body within inches of me. I would have given anything to be with him, but I was afraid of losing what was by far the most important relationship in my life.

But regardless of my fear, every Friday night, the same thing would happen. Pretending to roll over, I'd move closer to his sleeping body, moving the covers somewhat off of us as I did. Even in the darkened room, I could see our pale bodies, side by side, my thigh against his. I could feel the hair on his leg brushing mine. As I lay there, I would slowly move my hand, a mere inch or two above his body, slowly moving down his torso, making my way to his cock. I could see it there, beckoning to me, half erect, lying across his thigh, his testicles nestled between his thighs. I would gently lay my hand on it, feeling it fight back against my hand's pressure, pushing up in stimulation, its thickness and warmth registering in my palm. My heart was pounding now, so loudly that I couldn't believe that the sound pulsing in my ears wasn't so loud as to wake Derek. But the incessant beating of my heart, nor my hand resting on his hard cock, nor my thigh against his, seemed to wake him.

Once I had placed my hand firmly on his cock, I would wait, maybe five, maybe ten minutes, before I slowly wrapped my fingers around his hard cock, using my other hand to free my own hard cock from its underwear prison. At times I would slowly move his foreskin back and forth, a pearl of pre-cum forming on the head of his dick, as I would jack myself more quickly. I would lean over, thinking about taking his cock in my mouth, getting so close that I could smell his testicles, a mixture of sweat and semen and musk.

One night, while playing with his dick, I rolled over onto my stomach and realized that my own hard cock had come to rest on Derek's open palm. I felt his hand close on my cock as I moved to take the tip of his cock into my mouth. I heard him slightly mutter "no" as he rolled over, pulling his arm from under my body, turning loose of my cock, and moving his own cock out of reach.

I panicked, and quickly turned away, lying flat on my back. After a few minutes of silence, and the return of his steady, deep breathing, I quietly rolled out of the bed and lay on the floor next to the bed. I slowly jerked myself off, smelling his scent on my hand. I smeared my cum off my hand and onto the bedspread and I crawled back into bed, feeling guilty.

I pulled the sheets up over both of us, feeling a chill from the AC. I so wanted to hold on to him, to smell the back of his neck, to feel his buttocks push back against me. As I lay there, Derek pushed his thigh back against mine, rolling slightly, letting his arm fall across my chest. He didn't say a word, assumingly still asleep. It was so good and yet so sad.

—David, 44

someone and to have that person care for you is an important human survival instinct. And that instinct is so essential to humans that, without it, even today, we die. Literally. Quickly at times, by suicide, or slowly at other times, through destructive behaviors like drinking, smoking, or unsafe sex. Even if we don't intentionally try to kill ourselves, without love we kill ourselves *emotionally*. There is plenty of evidence of the effects of living without love. We see a higher incidence of unhappiness and more physical illness among those who report not being in a happy relationship. Sadly, some of us are convinced that we can live alone, divorcing ourselves from family, friends, and even at times society as a whole. Unabomber Ted Kaczynski comes to mind.

IS THERE SOMEONE FOR EVERYONE?

No. There will always be people who are so mentally unstable as to be unable to maintain a healthy relationship (although I have seen people I thought could never maintain a relationship rise to the occasion). The bottom line is this: men who want a lifelong love can find it.

Though currently it may seem difficult for gay men to form long-term relationships, there are exceptions. I know because I am one. On September 21, 2007, my partner and I celebrated twenty-two years together. Our years together have brought us one incredible experience after another, including two of the most memorable events in my life: our wedding and the christening of our adopted son. That's not to say there have not been difficult challenges; there have been plenty. But we have always faced them together. *Together* is a powerful word.

THE NATURE OF LOVE

Love is a *natural* human experience that we all hold in common. Love is love is love, to paraphrase Gertrude Stein, be it gay or straight. We know, primarily through the study of heterosexuals, that human love relationships are not magical, mysterious experiences—love doesn't come to us like lottery winnings, each of us buying a ticket, hoping that this time maybe we'll win. Love is a natural, organic process, a means of accomplishing survival of the species, with a long evolutionary history of pleasure and joy and reproduction and safety and security all playing a role in its success. And unlike the lottery, we all play along, without even a conscious decision to play— every man and woman, gay and straight, every day.

So why are some gay men able to form happy relationships, while others struggle? Why are some of us able to find our Superman in plain clothes, while many just end up sleeping with sexy, but forever single, Lex Luther, over and over again? Perhaps the best place to start in our search for answers about gay relationships is nature. Birds do it, bees do it, and humans have been doing it for millennia.

Part II

IN WHICH WE LEARN
HOW EVOLUTION
INFLUENCES MATING,
DATING, AND FEELINGS
OF LOVE

As our story continues, we find our hero searching for answers to his growing discomfort, to know the source of his darkness. He scans the ancient texts of the Xeria library, consults with the soothsayers at tKzenn, and visits the readers of runes at Thebes.

CHAPTER 2

What Drove Wolverine into the Arms of Layla Miller Instead of into the Bed of Cyclops? The Psychobiology of Evolutionary Mating

RARELY DO THE WORLDS of romance and science cross paths. Too bad, because they are intrinsically linked: romance could not happen without science. They might seem an odd couple—a romantic leading man on the arm of the bespectacled geek—but there is no denying that human romance is an evolutionary tool to assure the survival of the species. I cannot put this more bluntly: love is a pimp, the front man for most human sexual encounters. In our search for clues to the how and why of successful gay love relationships, going to the source, human mating, is the first step.

Earlier, we noted that gay men tend to find themselves not in lifelong relationships but in series of relatively short, five-year relationships, with growing spaces of time between those relationships. While many may feel that modern humans are free from instinct, and gay men in particular are free from *reproductive* instincts, many scientists believe that humans are not the least instinctual animal, but actually *the most*. Gay men are obviously and strongly driven by sex, despite the reproductive futility of their sex drive. Does this mean that gay men are biologically destined to be stuck in a series of short-term, declining relationships, each one becoming harder to establish as we age? No.

What it means is that those men who ignore the biological and instinctual factors that come into play when two men form a relationship, and then fail to understand and manage those instinctual factors, are most likely to follow the same short-term relationship path. Fortunately, those gay men who desire a lifelong relationship have other options.

But there may be some obstacles along the way. If we want lifelong love, we have to acknowledge the power of biology that enables all relationships, gay and straight, to work. The human mating process allows heterosexual relationships not only to survive, but to thrive. This same process allows lesbian women to naturally form long-term relationships. So why do gay men have such a hard time? What is in their nature that allows, or assists, heterosexual and lesbian relationships to survive? The most obvious element missing from gay marriages when compared to successful straight and lesbian marriages is, well, *women*. Now that's an interesting clue.

Women? Surely, you must think I'm kidding. I can hear it now, "Is this guy saying we have to be *women* to be happily married?" Well, some of us. Maybe a better choice of words would be feminine. Gentle men?

Stay with me for a minute—and consider this solely as a theory at this point. Is it possible that all successful relationships are dependent on a counterbalancing phenomenon, a balancing of the masculine and the feminine? This is certainly the concept behind the ancient Chinese philosophy of yin and yang, which assumes that all life is a combination of complementing energies, such as light and dark, hot and cold, and in relationships, *masculine and feminine*.

If it *is* necessary for such counterbalancing energies to be

"'I'd die for you.' Powerful words, yes, but words of love story fantasies. Are they true for the gays? In the world of superheroes, yes, maybe, but homosexuals, well…" She paused, looking at me with a sense of sadness, my truth glaringly on display. "I don't think so, dear."

I was devastated. Bored in class, I had been caught by the teacher reading *The Front Runner,* a love story of a male Olympic athlete and his (also male) coach. In 1976, it was very controversial. In an attempt to embarrass me, she asked me to describe what I was reading to the class. When I got to the part where the story's heroes said they were willing to die for each other's love, the room erupted in laughter and moans.

I refused to believe her. These men, while they may be fictional, were very real to me. They gave me hope that my life could be good, that I could find a real man to love. I wanted to believe that two men could have not only sex but also love. And I didn't want some frustrated love affair, hidden away shamefully, but an honest marriage. I would be the Olympic runner Billy Sieve, and one day my Harlan Brown would find me. And I'd be so in love with him that I would die for him. I joined the track team later that year, convinced that I'd find some Alpha male, some masculine coach to spend my life with.

—*Carlos, 54*

present for a relationship to function over the long run, heterosexual relationships certainly are well equipped—after all, men and women *are* different. But what about the high success rate of lesbian relationships? They would appear to be a contradiction of our theory—but think about the easy interplay between the masculine and the feminine in lesbian relation-

I hate queens. I hate those men who lisp about, like they're butterflies. They turn my stomach. And such bitches, too! You ask me what I hate about gay men, it's that. Those guys think they're all that, hot shit and all. They're queens, nothing more, silly little girls.

—*Perry, 27*

ships. The lesbian community takes great joy in celebrating all things feminine, while at the same time embracing the more liberating aspects of today's feminism, such as the right to be women in traditional male roles.

This certainly isn't true in the gay community. Ask almost any gay man if he likes others to think of him as feminine and I assure you he'll say no. Most gay men, to say the least, do not value femininity. In our community's rush to worship at the altar of masculinity, we have not only banned femininity to a great degree; we have also thereby lost the essential counterbalancing formula for relationships.

So, does the counterbalancing-trait theory hold water? Possibly, if for no other reason than that human relationships are based on a *sexual* reproduction system. It is a system naturally inclined to support a mating of differences. But what's this got to do with gay *love* relationships? Let's not forget that love is simply the pimp, getting people to mate, so they can reproduce. And there is no significant difference in the love gay men feel and the love everyone else feels. Even if we consciously don't want to be involved in such a mating system, our shared evolutionary history means we have to deal with this sexual mating system.

But let's not jump to the next level yet. I know it's rare for a gay guy to say he wants to marry a woman, or even a highly feminine man. But that's not to say there is no form of difference between the men who form successful gay marriages. Not to give away anything, but here's our second clue: Do you remember the personal ad at the beginning of the Introduction, Superhero in Search of Sidekick?

LOVE AS CHEMISTRY

In order for us to truly consider our theory that there could be a necessary yin/yang dynamic in healthy gay relationships, we must first understand that love is a *biological* process, as opposed to an emotional experience—not a very romantic idea and often hard for us to believe. It just doesn't feel like love is a couple of hundred thousand neurons firing in response to a flood of neurochemicals we call hormones. Most of us want to believe in a love that is red roses and moonlit walks and soft kisses. Of course, love is both. The first is the mechanical process; the second is the *experience* of that mechanical process. And we can artificially trigger those *feelings* of being in love by artificially stimulating the system, just as it happens when one is high on Ecstasy, but without the harmful side effects.

Often the science is hidden behind our desire for magic. Such is the nature of consciousness: we feel as if we are fully aware of what we are thinking and doing, even when we are being guided by eons of evolution.

A main concept of evolutionary psychology is the presence of *universal traits*, behaviors and decision-making processes

---

Listen, Ellen, I've been doing some thinking over the last couple of months... about my Animal Man powers and stuff... and, well, I've come to a decision. I want to go full time into the super-hero business. But, as for marriage, well… it goes against my animal instincts.

—*Buddy Baker, aka Animal Man, DC Comics*

My first date was with a girl at my school who I was completely uninterested in. She stood five eight, a good three inches taller than me, and was at least 100 pounds heavier than me. I remember her name was Peggy, not because I recall names well, but because I remember she was always teased, others calling her "Piggy." As is often the case with put-downs, there was an element of truth to this one. With her turned-up nose and prominent nostrils, I'm sad to say she did have a slight resemblance to a pig.

I had no desire to go to my junior high prom, but my parents insisted. And I especially didn't want to go with Peggy. I wanted to go with David. But now, against my wishes, I stood in my pale blue seersucker suit, next to this Amazon of a young woman. We looked for the entire world like Jack Sprat and his wife. I felt that she would eat me alive, like some human variation on the mating habits of the praying mantis, even though I had not even the slightest desire to mate with her.

From some back bedroom emerged my date, looking huge, and as if she had been stuffed into a dress that her mother had made, all baby blue satin. Her hair was done up in the style of the day, known as Grecian curls. We stood for pictures, both mothers holding Instamatic

that occur consistently in humans, regardless of culture or geographical location, and that facilitate the survival of the species. In *Psychoanalytic, Ethological, and Sociobiological Theories*, the evolutionary psychology researcher Bernard Weiner developed a test to examine such universal traits, based on behaviors that we have traditionally considered rational or cameras, their flashcubes popping. Peggy stood next to me, overpowering in both her girth and height.

I had never felt more uncomfortable, that is, until my mother pulled out a corsage of blue-dyed carnations and baby's breath. I was shaking as Peggy bent over for me to pin it on her. Her breasts grew larger, filling her satin top, as she leaned down so I could reach her. I slipped my hand inside her dress, feeling her bra strap against her skin as I heard my father behind me make some lewd comment about "not being in there for too long…" Somehow, the corsage stayed in place despite my shaking and my growing repulsion for the whole evening.

After the insistence of more photos ("Kiss! Kiss her!" the mothers had urged), we were off to the school in the back of my father's Chevy Impala. I got out and opened the door for Peggy. As we were heading in, my father called her back to the car, placing something in her white-gloved hand. When she returned, I asked her what he had said. She blankly opened her hand to reveal a crumpled ten-dollar bill. "All he said was, 'Thanks, thanks for helping us out…'" How much shame can be bought with a ten-dollar bill?

—*Mathew, 47*

emotional choices but that theorists believe to be universal to the human species. Many of Weiner's test questions reflect our hard wiring when it comes to decisions we make about reproduction. Here's an example. Answer this question honestly: Who would you grieve more, the death of a healthy child or the death of a child with an obvious genetic disability?

When I ask my students to answer this question with a show of hands, most say they would grieve equally the deaths of these two children. But, asked to vote anonymously, virtually 100 percent say they would be saddened more by the death of the healthy child. Why? Evolutionary psychologists say it is because the existence of a genetically damaged child could endanger the species. If such a child were able to survive long enough to reproduce, and thus pass on the genetic disability to future generations, the species would be genetically weaker and would result in a less reproductive lineage.

Interesting, yes, and it seems to point out that behind our thinking, quite often a biological history is at play. But the point I want to make with this experiment is that *everyone* says they would grieve the death of a healthy child more than the death of an unhealthy child—even (nonsexually reproducing) gay men. It appears that gay men, just like everyone else, carry remnants of that evolutionary mating biology; otherwise, it would seem that we wouldn't care which child lived or died. Our shared evolution pulls all of us under the same umbrella of survival drives, even the drive to reproduce, even when it is irrelevant.

As much as we may want to consciously override such instincts, it rarely works. If you have ever tried to stop being gay, you know it's impossible. Some of our deepest and most powerful brain wiring is involved in mate selection. Throughout the human species we see hundreds, if not hundreds of thousands, of indicators of such evolutionary guidance in mate-selection behaviors—in particular, in what we find attractive in our potential mates. These are called *mating strategies*. For heterosexuals, these attractive traits are, of course, different: men tend to find women and their bodies and behaviors attractive, and women tend to find the bodies and behaviors of men attractive.

Which brings us to an essential question: What do gay men find attractive? Do we all like the same things? I'd say no. Do all gay men display the same mating behaviors to draw mates? Again, I'd say no, but it has been the assumption of most people that all gay men want the same thing in a mate and act the same way to get it. Do gay men find other men attractive in the same way heterosexual women do, or do we seek partners with the traits that heterosexual men use to find mates? Are we more like men or women? In order for us to fully understand the mating choices of gay men, we have to know what the mating choices of men and women are.

WHAT HETEROSEXUAL MEN WANT, WHAT HETEROSEXUAL WOMEN WANT

The traits that men seek in women and women seek in men, and the manner in which we draw those people to us, are, as we pointed out earlier, mating strategies. And these human mating strategies come in two versions: a male version and a female version. Men and women are biologically and psychologically designed, and are expected by society, to express desire via different mating strategies. As an example, women who are sexually aggressive generally are seen as inappropriate, whereas men who are not sexually aggressive enough are seen as somehow "off."

Many heterosexual human mating strategies were catalogued for the first time in 1994, when Dr. David Buss conducted a worldwide survey to determine whether there was a pattern of universal mating strategies for men and women. It seems that men, in general, find women attractive if they appear to be young, healthy, and fertile. Buss found that women whose waists are roughly a third narrower than their hips are considered the most attractive.

Our ancient ancestors determined who was healthiest by the means they had: physical appearance and lively behavior. And men still seek women with traits that indicate health and vitality, such as full lips, clear, smooth skin, clear eyes, shiny hair, and good muscle tone. Emotionally, men prefer women who are lively and have a youthful gait, an animated facial expression, and a high energy level. Additionally, men prefer spouses who are of reproductive age and younger than they are. Since a woman's reproductive capability declines markedly as she approaches the age of forty, it is little surprise that some men seek younger women as outside sex partners as their wives age.

In these mating traits of heterosexual men, we can certainly see some of the same characteristics that gay men seek in a partner. Many gay men prefer partners who are younger, vital, with an athletic, muscular body. But what about the other half of these couples, those gay men who prefer men who are older than they are and who focus less on their partner's physical appearance and characteristics? Are these mating traits more commonly seen among heterosexual women?

It is true that women tend to prefer mates who are older than they are, and also focus less on a man's physical attractiveness than on his ability to provide safety and resources. A man's physical appearance does provide clues to his ability to provide for a partner, including signs of premature graying being appealing as a sign of maturity, broad shoulders being a sign of physical health and ability to dominate others, and nice clothing and good teeth being an essential sign of affluence. Women are also drawn to men who display a higher level of testosterone, as evidenced by a strong jawline, a heavier beard, and a traditional V-shaped back, all traits of men who historically were reproductive and fertile defenders and providers. It's no accident that Superman and Batman both have these very characteristics!

As in the past, women continue to look for men who have adequate resources for ensuring the future success of their offspring. This is why men with power and money, regardless of their physical attractiveness, are generally able to have their pick of beautiful women. Power, in all it forms—physical, social, and financial—is attractive to women. As Henry Kissinger is known for saying, "Power is the greatest aphrodisiac."

I can also see many of these traditional female mating strategies among gay men. I know plenty of men who find a heavy beard and a square jaw attractive. I also can name quite a few personal friends who find comfort in knowing that they will be provided for by their partners, in case they are unable to care for themselves.

It appears that gay men use a variety of mating strategies, some male and some female, in their pursuit of life partners. I guess my question at this point is, Do some gay men use more of the female strategies, while other gay men use more traditional male strategies? We certainly see variations in masculine and feminine behaviors among gay men, an indication of some bimodal mating strategy at work. We know that masculine and feminine behaviors are organic devices for attracting mates, and thus are deeply based within the limbic system of the brain.

Speaking of the brain, while the vast majority of differences we see between men and women are within the reproductive systems of the body, we should not be surprised that there are small, yet significant differences in certain structures of men's and women's brains, since the brain plays a key function in all sexual and mating situations.

For example, men are generally better at imagining three-dimensional objects, a skill known as mental rotation. Men are also better at perceiving and judging spatial relationships and at targeting and intercepting objects that are moving on a trajectory, skills used in such mundane daily tasks as catching a baseball and parallel parking. Priding themselves in finding their way about in novel environments is such a male-identified trait that, when it fails, it often becomes the butt of a joke: "Honey, why don't you just stop and ask directions?"

Women, on the other hand, tend to have superior skills in

their ability to ace tests of verbal fluency, to excel in skills of coding and of perceptual speed, and to remember the locations of previously seen objects. Women also tend to be better at social interactions and with both verbal and nonverbal communication. Women are especially skilled at reading emotional cues. Such traits explain the higher number of women in certain professions, including psychology and teaching.

When considering these traits with gay men in mind, again we see certain men who fit the classic male style, while others seem to have more in common with women.

IN THE BRAIN

The differences we see between men and women, and any differences we see between gay men and heterosexual men, originate in brain structure. The organic basis for so much of who we are, how we act and react, and the source of most mating strategies lies deep within the human brain, in a section called the limbic system. The limbic system is highly involved in regulating both physical and psychological functions. Specific parts of the limbic system, mainly the amygdala and the hypothalamus, are closely involved in regulating emotions, especially emotions related to mating behaviors. These two tiny little structures play a major role in our love lives, influencing emotional reactions as well as our basic drives for food and sex. The limbic system plays a key role in defining what makes us men or women, as well as what makes us gay or straight. Obviously, the sexual behaviors of gay men are different from those of heterosexual men, simply by their choice of sex partners.

Sexual desire is only one of many personality traits tied to the limbic system. An amazing number of traits that define us, including traits that we may generally assume to be within our control, are actually strongly influenced by our biology. For example, our degree of aggressiveness or passivity; our balance between masculinity and femininity; our optimism or pessimisim; even our desires for a mate, for children, and for social acceptance fall within the influence of the limbic system.

As we delve more deeply into the how and why of successful gay relationships, with brain structure being such an obviously important piece of the puzzle, we have to answer the question of universal similarities or differences in the physical bodies and brains of gay men. You may be familiar with a breakthrough research study conducted by Simon LeVay on the brain structures of gay men. The headlines tended to read something like this: "Gay Men's Hypothalamuses Built Like Women's." If, in fact, *all* gay men's brains are built in certain ways like those of women's, why do we see behavioral differences between masculine gay men and feminine gay men? And, secondarily, if we do see consistent results for gay men's brain structures, the whole idea of two mating styles is completely out the window—we can't act two different ways if we all have one brain design. We need to know more about how gay men's bodies, and brains, are built, because that is where we'll find our most important clue.

"You mean to tell me you've been married to her for fifteen years?...And they call me Superman!"

—George Reeves to Desi Arnaz, *I Love Lucy*

CHAPTER 3

Brain Boy Compares Notes with the Incredible Hulk: The Physiology of the Gay Body and Brain

In 1962, Matt and Mary Price's car blows a tire and swerves off the road, hitting an electrical pole. Both Matt and Mary are electrocuted, yet only Matt is killed. Mary, six months pregnant at the time of the accident, later gives birth to a son. She names him after his father. As she talks to the newborn, he answers her in perfect English. He would later grow up to be a superhero and an agent for the United States Secret Service, fighting crime and going by the name Brain Boy.

—Internationalhero.com

THE HEADLINES ABOUT the recent discoveries concerning the bodies and brains of gay men always seem a bit sensational—and universal in the belief that all gay men are alike ("Gay men this…" or "Gay men that…"). Rarely is it noted that some of the gay men studied did not have the observed trait. And overwhelmingly, the research indicates that when there is a difference between gay and heterosexual men, the gay men exhibit feminized traits.

So what? As we have seen earlier, the physical design of men and women—in the obvious differences between men's

I had a best friend when I was in elementary school. We did everything together. One day, we were skinny dipping at my parents' lakehouse and my friend got an erection. I was sort of excited by that, but afraid at the same time. I didn't say anything, thinking it was just the cold water that had caused him to get hard. That night he slept over. I had two twin beds in my room there. He slept in one, I slept in the other. I woke up in the middle of the night realizing he had snuck into my bed. I looked at him, his face in the moonlight, he was an angel sleeping. When I realized that I was getting hard looking at him, I panicked. I got angry and pushed him out of my bed, waking him up with a start. He begged me, crying almost, to let him sleep with me. I told him I wasn't queer. The next day I couldn't look at him. He went home a day early, his folks coming to get him. I was relieved, but, later, I jerked off thinking about his hard cock.

—Ned, 30

and women's reproductive systems and between their brains' mating functions—is reflected in distinct mating strategies. The assumption that all gay men are basically the same when it comes to mating style also assumes that all gay men are the same in physical body and brain design as well. But something isn't right here. There are obvious differences when it comes to gay men's behaviors—some are more feminine and others are more masculine—so it only makes sense that there have to be differences in the brain structures that manage gay mating behaviors. Does research indicate gay men are all the same or different? The success of long-term gay relationships could depend on the answer to this simple question.

ARE THERE DIFFERENCES AMONG GAY MEN?

Researchers have only begun to look at this question and, honestly, most research has focused not on gay mating strategies but on finding a universal marker of homosexuality. Yet even in these studies, if we look at the data gathered, we can find evidence that indicates that gay men do come with varying biological structures that could influence mating strategies.

We have lots of anecdotal evidence that such differences exist: plenty of gay men exhibit feminine behaviors, behaviors we associate with female mating, and plenty behave in a masculine manner. There have to be some differences in the brain's development to result in such variations in behavior. And there are.

In 1991, Simon LeVay discovered that homosexual and heterosexual men have a difference in size in the third interstitial nuclei of the hypothalamic anterior. The size of the hypothalamic nuclei determines the gender that the fetus will find attractive as an adult. Simply put, those people with larger hypothalamus nuclei are attracted to women and those with smaller nuclei are attracted to men, regardless of their own gender. But the sizes of the hypothalamic nuclei varied within the gay group as well, with some of the subjects' nuclei being similar in size to those of the heterosexual men. If hypothalamic nuclei size is indicative of sexual orientation, then this research fails to prove that.

It does indicate something completely different, though. We know that the hypothalamus is a key player in mating behaviors. Could these differences be indicative of differences in the mating strategies being employed by these gay men? In

"If you could be any superhero, who would you be?"

"I don't know. Silver Surfer, probably. I'd like to be able to fly around," I said.

"I'd be Batman. He's cool, his car's cool. Plus he's rich. Hey, you could be Robin. He has a cool motorcycle, and we could live together in Bruce Wayne's mansion."

He lay there, half in and half out of his sleeping bag, his bare leg on top of the olive drab military surplus bag his folks had picked up at some garage sale. His pale skin barely lighted by the weakening flashlight, I could see the dark hair on his shins and a strip of his white briefs showing on his thigh. He was two years older than me, but we were both at about the same stage of development. His bare chest showed his pecs, far stronger than mine. My chest, as he pointed out, was a "pirate's delight"—a sunken chest. He also took pride in his "treasure trail," the line of hair that started at his belly button and made its way to his crotch. Earlier, he'd pulled his briefs down to show off his thickening patch of dark brown pubic fuzz. He fingered the hair for a second, before he popped his waistband back into place, never showing me his dick.

For Cam, masculinity was his world, intrinsic to his nature. For me, the opposite was true, and my differ-

other words, were the gay men who had hypothalamic nuclei similar to women's also using feminine mating strategies, while the gay men whose hypothalamic nuclei were similar to men using masculine mating strategies?

ADDITIONAL EVIDENCE

There is an overwhelming body of evidence that supports the idea that gay men have specific developmental similarities *with women*. In particular, research into gay men's bodies tends to

ences were obvious to those around me. A day didn't pass when it wasn't noted, usually in anger, that I threw like a girl, or cried too much, or that I was a "faggot."

The flashlight flickered, then went dead. The darkness of the tent, the quiet of the night, it was as if we weren't there anymore, as if we were floating. I reached out toward Cam's sleeping bag and unintentionally touched his face, gently, then his leg, feeling the hair on his thigh. I left my hand there for a second longer than I should have, but Cam didn't pull away. "Sorry, I was just checking to see if you were there," I said.

"I'm always here," he answered. My heart ached. As much as I wanted to believe him, I didn't. He wouldn't be there.

I rolled over in the dark, my dick rock hard. I wanted Cam to reach out and put his arms around me, to hold me. I wanted so badly at that moment to be Robin to his Batman. I wanted to be by his side forever, to bask in his glory, making sure he had what he needed to succeed, assuring me that he'd be there for me forever as well. I would have done anything for him.

—David, 23

show key differences from the bodies of heterosexual men in those areas of the body that develop during the third trimester, the period when androgen levels *in utero* play their biggest role. For example, the majority of gay men have longer penises than heterosexual men, distinctive fingerprint patterns, different walking gaits, more defined auditory mechanisms of the inner ear, unique hair-growth patterns, and distinctively shorter upper leg bones and forearm bones.

Gay men's bodies also reflect variations in androgen stimulation in their outward appearance. A key marker of androgen variation is seen in the ratio of the second digit to the fourth digit—the length of the pointer finger compared to the ring finger. In most gay men, these finger lengths reflect the feminization of the male body that occurs during fetal development. Most heterosexual men have a second finger (the "pointer" finger) that is shorter and stubbier than their fourth finger, but women tend to have second and fourth fingers of the same length. We know that higher levels of androgens result in the male-typical pattern, whereas lower levels of androgens result in a female-typical pattern. Finger-length ratio, like the development of the hypothalamus, occurs during the beginning of the third trimester of pregnancy. Thus, it isn't surprising to see that gay men also tend to display a second-digit-to-fourth-digit ratio similar to that of women.

In fact, the majority of gay men tend to have general body differences that indicate a feminization of the male body. Gay men tend to have shorter femurs, as women do, and have female-like fingerprints, female-like gaits, and female-like hourglass-shaped bodies. The feminized traits continue to stack up as more and more research is conducted. And not only do we see these differences in the physical structures of gay men's bodies, we also see similar results in mental skill abilities, in tasks where we normally see differences between men and women.

In their exhaustive book, *Born Gay: The Psychobiology of Sex Orientation*, two leading psychologists in the field of human sexuality, Drs. Glenn Wilson and Qazi Rahman, discuss the concept of a gay brain:

> *[W]e have considered some of the genetic and prenatal mechanisms by which sexual orientation may arise. Clearly, whatever the precise mechanism, these influences must have their effects on the developing brain of the "pre-*

heterosexual" or "pre-homosexual" individual forming in the womb. After all, it is the brain that generates all our behavior (not some wisp behind our heads called "the mind" that we carry with us like a balloon).

How do gay men perform on such neuropsychological tests? The answers are not clear-cut, but a predominance of research results from almost all tests of cognitive function indicate that the vast majority (between 70 and 75 percent) of gay men had cognitive functions similar to women's. As a result, we often hear statements that gay men's brains have developed in a manner closer to the design of a woman's brain in these specific cognitive skills.

There are literally hundreds of research projects recently published or currently under review that have confirmed what many gay men have been told throughout their lives: you throw like a girl, you run like a girl, you act like a girl. But now there is evidence of a biological basis for this. Our question, of course, is, How does this all affect our mating skills? Does this evidence of a biological basis for feminization of our bodies and brains require us to add to the list: throw like girl, run like a girl, think like a girl, *mate like a girl?*

I don't want to be a girl. I, like so many gay men, have fought long and hard at not fitting into the gay stereotypes. Like so many other gay men, I, too, carry the scars of a youth of being called sissy. But there is no denying that research is indicating a biological basis for some gay men, in fact the majority of gay men, being feminized by androgen flux in utero.

Yet the thing that sticks in my mind is that, while there may be a majority of gay men who are biologically feminized in some way, there is always a group of gay men *who are not.* If this is the case, why would we think all gay men mate alike?

There is another nagging question: Where do bisexual men fit into this mating picture?

"I read about the Kinsey scale when I was in graduate school in the sixties. I quickly identified myself as a bisexual. I had sex with a woman in undergraduate school and really enjoyed it. Later, when I went into the seminary, the term 'bisexual' was easier for me to reconcile with my religious views—at least I had not sinned completely in God's eyes; I could still be saved." [Edward laughed, his blue eyes twinkling.] "What I had ignored, though, was I hadn't had sex with a woman since, instead having sex with only men—and loving it. And speaking of love, I never felt the love for a woman the way I felt for a man. I still see myself as bisexual. Even now, at sixty-seven, I see women I could have sex with. Sex with, not marry. Oh God, no. I know clearly that I prefer to be with another man for life—sex isn't all there is to life!"

—Edward, 67

THE PUZZLE OF BISEXUALITY

Why would the presence of bisexuals be a problem when we're searching for the basis of successful *gay* relationships? Because theoretically, the presence of true male bisexuality, in which we assume some men are *hard-wired* to find both genders equally attractive, is in direct conflict with the argument that there is a biological basis for sexuality and male and female

MY SUPERHERO BODY IS IN MY OTHER T-SHIRT

—*Seen on a T-shirt*

I can't see anyone more than once. I don't like men who have even the slightest hint of femininity. As soon as I see they are even a little bit queeny, I'm turned off. And honestly, it's getting harder and harder to meet men. I started out going out with gay guys, but got turned off when they would want to kiss. No real man wants to kiss another guy. I then started seeing only bi guys, but found most of them to be gay inside. I then started going to dark sex bars to suck guys, but eventually one would open his mouth, and I could tell he was feminine. For a while, I hung out at the baths, hooking up with straight guys sneaking out on their wives, until one of them started screaming that he "loved" me while I was fucking him. "Enough of that, girly," I said. Since then, I have been just hanging out in a glory hole I know about. Trust me, no one's cock looks feminine. After all, nothing is more male than a cock, huh?

—Jacques, 44

[I can't help but notice that Jacques licks his lips as he talks about "cock." Licking one's lips is a classic mating strategy—a classic *female* mating strategy.]

mating behaviors. Few genetic traits are expressed on a spectrum. Genetic information generally is expressed in an "on or off" manner. The concept of male bisexuality appears to be primarily a response to social stigma. I say this with such confidence because of the amazing amount of scientific research that supports such a position. While scientists have found a substantial population of men who *claim* to be attracted to both men and women to some degree, when measured scientifically, their bisexuality tends to morph into homosexuality.

In 1993, the psychologist and sex researcher Mike Bailey

As I entered my teen years, there was a general increase in the discussion of sexuality in America. The publication of the book *Everything You Wanted to Know About Sex* But Were Afraid to Ask* and the increased visibility of the gay community after the Stonewall riots coincided with the growing sexual revolution. I first heard the word "gay" when I was probably ten or eleven. It was always associated with negativity and, in particular, with feminine men. The words "faggot," "homo," and "queer" were much more commonly heard, especially in my world. The message I received was being gay meant being a boy who wanted to be a girl. But I didn't feel like a girl, or even think of myself as a girl. But for some reason, my body did seem to be a boy's body with some attitudes and behaviors commonly seen in girls my age. I did throw like an unathletic girl, I did run like an awkward girl, I did enjoy the company of girls over boys my age, and I did prefer my sister's Barbie Dreamhouse over my GI Joe jeep.

I found there were other guys, also feminine like me, who were also interested in sex with other guys. And at times I did have sex with some of them, but I felt little emotional attraction to them. At the same time I was

at the University of Chicago conducted a research project that shed some light on the question of bisexuality in men. Bailey and his colleagues gathered a group of 120 men, of whom one-third identified as solely homosexual, one-third identified solely as heterosexual, and one-third identified as bisexual. Each subject was attached to a penile plethysmograph, a device designed to measure increase in girth and volume of the penis as it becomes aroused. The subjects were shown one of two erotic films, either two men engaged in sexual activity or two fooling around with other feminine guys, I pined away for the same boys that most of the girls in school pined for: school jock David, class clown Steve, and above all, our math teacher, Mr. Boone. His five o'clock shadow drove me to such distraction that still today, when a fraction problem comes up, I find myself sexually aroused. [He laughs.]

Yet all the guys I fooled around with weren't feminine. In fact, these guys were often the most masculine boys in class. And for some reason I didn't understand, it was these guys, the masculine ones, for whom I fell head over heels in love. Was this simply a reaction, a type of internalized homophobia, disliking men who were feminine, or was there some special attraction to these guys? Not that it mattered. No matter how hard I tried to get these guys to love me back, for whatever reason, they wouldn't or couldn't do it. Sex, yes; love, no. But I couldn't help but wonder, What was the story with these guys? Were they gay like me, or were they just experimenting? Did they feel the same way toward me, but couldn't express it because of social pressure or religious beliefs? Or were these guys just adolescents experimenting?

—Andrew, 48

women engaged in sexual activity. Heterosexual images were not included because it would be impossible to determine which sex partner the subject found arousing.

Bailey's results showed, as expected, that heterosexual men were aroused by the images of two women having sex. As was also expected, the gay subjects found the gay sex images arousing. What was surprising to the researchers were the reactions of the men who identified themselves as bisexual. These subjects found only the material with the two men arousing, and had little reaction to the film of the two women.

This may seem like a small detail, but I have to ask, If every man in the world who claimed to be bisexual came out and started dating and marrying gay men instead of women, would we be having such a hard time finding good mates? Are these bisexual men actually the masculine gay men who don't show up in the research results? As we shall see in future chapters, the lack of true bisexuality in the male community plays a key role in finding an appropriate mate for many gay men.

THE 70/30 SPLIT

Reconsidering all the evidence of differences between gay men and heterosexual men, one begins to notice what has to be our most obvious clue. Like so many before me, I had fallen into the trap of assuming gay men are all alike, that the majority results reflect the true nature of all gay men. But the word "majority" doesn't mean everyone—in fact, it means most, and as such confirms something we've suspected. If we see a study indicating that a *majority* of gay men have a specific trait, we can just as easily be assured that a *minority* of gay men *do not* have that trait.

In study after study, a significant pattern appears: a majority of the gay test subjects, usually around 70 percent, do display signs of androgen feminization, but *approximately 30 percent do not*. In other words, while all the test subjects are gay, only 70 percent present with the so-called "gay trait." Were some of the gay test subjects "more gay" than the others?

The presence of these physical differences indicates that sexual orientation is not involved in this process of androgen variation in utero, just the *degree of expression* of the trait. If we see these androgen-related differences in the development of gay men's bodies, wouldn't we also see differences in the expression of mating behaviors that are dictated by these structures? Time

> Catwoman: I could give you more happiness than anyone in the world.
>
> Batman: How do you propose to do that?
>
> Catwoman: By being your partner in life—I mean, it's me and you against the world.
>
> Batman: What about Robin?
>
> Catwoman: Hmmm.... I know. We'll kill him.
>
> — *"Batman Displays His Knowledge,"*
> Batman *TV Show*

and again, studies reveal, on average, the 70/30 split, in which the majority of the gay subjects displayed signs of feminization of the brain, but 30 percent not only scored in a masculine manner, but well within the norms for heterosexual men.

The implications of the 70/30 split are profound. Right under our noses is strong evidence that there are two different types of gay men, *biologically different*: the Alpha gay male and the Beta gay male. And these differences do not occur in some mundane area of life, but in the very area we are concerned with: mating behaviors. Is it possible that we have uncovered a gay version of the larger evolutionary mating system? If we have, we have found a system that, if understood, could result in every gay man finding love as easily as falling off a log—it's that natural.

In addition, if this is so, not only will we have found the key to success in gay relationships, we may have found the explanation for hundreds of other mysteries in the gay community, from the heightened physical attention gay men give their bodies (a mating trait common to females in most societies) to the basis for the notorious gay "bitch" behaviors (a common defensive behavior that occurs when the male–female ratio of a society falls out of balance).

At this point we need to confirm our theory. We need to ask a few gay men about their mating behaviors. Would gay men choose to mate as women do, as men do, both, or neither? We'd know for sure we were on to something if our results showed the same 70/30 split, with most gay men following mating strategies of women and the rest following mating strategies of men. Of course, there was the other possibility of finding gay men's answers all over the place. If that was the case, we'd be back at square one.

Part III

IN WHICH WE ASK GAY MEN
WHAT THEY WANT
AND NEED

With dark loneliness growing throughout the world, our hero calls together all with special powers to a universal summit at the Point where the Constellations Demitri and Mixto cross.

CHAPTER 4

Calling All Members of the Justice League: A National Survey of Gay Men

Questions? I'm sure millions of viewers...are wondering what it's like to wear the tights of justice. Well, it's tingly and it's uncomfortable.

—The Tick, a superhero, *The Tick TV Show*

IN THE SUMMER OF 2006, over two thousand gay men agreed to answer a 96-question survey concerning a wide variety of their sexual and emotional mating habits. Research specifically into the biological basis for male homosexuality is only beginning as we enter the twenty-first century. The earlier studies of gay men focused on a variety of issues, from acceptance of the mere existence of homosexuality to possible causation of same-gender attraction. Until recently, thought on homosexuality has been guided by conjecture, while scientific research has focused mainly on the sexual aspects of male homosexuality, failing to look at the more complex issues of male–male affectional relationships.

Although evolutionary psychology was one of the first scientific fields to take a serious look into the biological and historical evolutionary basis for human *romantic* behaviors, historically it has focused on heterosexual couples. It has only been in the last decade or so that researchers have taken a serious look at

"Do you like it?"

I had driven over an hour to a desolate doublewide trailer in a recently cleared patch of land. It was a cold February day, gray, overcast. I had turned sixteen five days earlier and gotten my driver's license. That Saturday afternoon, I borrowed my mother's car and headed south to try to understand an urge that was eating at me.

His name was Frank, the illegitimate son of a German woman and an American soldier, and he was maybe two years older than me. Frank's mother had married another American soldier and had immigrated with her new husband and her son to the United States. Her new husband was a member of the church, and that was how Frank and I met—in church.

He was feminine, smelled of body odor, had tight, curly blond hair all over his young body, and a face that wasn't all that great. But in him I saw a potential sex partner, a release for the urge that was driving me crazy. I hated that I needed him. I had sex with Frank, even though I didn't love him, or even want him that much. Was this to be a pattern in my future? I know so many gay men who say they grow bored with sex after getting into a relationship. Was this the same pattern?

Frank's adoptive father had given him the trailer, getting him out of his parents' house now that he was out of high school. I had driven down on a whim, knocking on the door, not knowing if he would be home or not. He looked out the lace curtain hung on the door's window and, seeing me, opened the door, asking me in. He didn't show any emotion, no smile, no grimace. He knew why I was there.

I walked in, noting to myself how low the ceiling was.

The room was hot in the center, cool near the windows. There was a small gas heater off to one side, hurriedly pouring heated air into the room just as quickly as it was sucked out of the poorly insulated mobile home.

I looked around at an assortment of secondhand furniture and German knickknacks. A large cardboard box held hundreds of comic books, some Little Lulu, some superheroes. I sat on the couch and asked if he was home alone as I began thumbing through the comic books. I noticed the superhero comics had pages stuck together. He answered "yes," he was alone. Never one for subtlety, I asked him if he wanted to suck me off. He hesitated.

"Do you like it?"

It seemed odd to me. He wanted to know that I, too, had the same weakness, the same aching need. He wanted to know if I was gay, too. I hated him at that moment—I didn't want in any way to be the same as he was. But the throbbing hard-on in my jeans wouldn't let me stop now. "Yeah," I said.

"No, really, do you like it, like guys who like other guys? Do you think it's the way we are? Do you think we were born gay?"

"Yeah, sure. I don't know. Why ask me? You want to fool around or not?"

He leaned over to kiss me. I turned away, instead reaching for his zipper, pulling his fat, short cock out. I played with it a bit, both aroused and repulsed by the scent coming from his crotch. He began to suck me while I played with his cock. Within a minute or two, not very long for sure, I began to shoot in his mouth, fighting his resistance. He gagged, turned and spat the cum into his hand. I zipped up, feeling the moistness of cum and spit in my shorts, the all too familiar wave of guilt flooding into my mind.

"You're gay, too, you know," he said to me. I'm nothing like you, I thought in my head. "Yeah, sure, whatever," I said in return. "You want me to get you off?" I asked, not wanting to. "No. Thanks. I can tell you don't want to." I felt bad, but at the same time the guilt I felt was driving me to the door, driving me to get away as fast as I could from him, from his scent, from what he had said about me.

That's my story. I guess what I want you to know now, and I wanted him to know then, is this: I am not gay. At least not gay like he is.

—*Ralph, 25*

the biology—the organic, innate basis—of homosexuality in all its complexity, addressing not only the sexual issues but also the more complex issues of social involvement, intimate love, and long-term relationships.

Though no universal gay trait has been located, researchers have found a wide variety of differences between gay men and heterosexual men, as we saw earlier. Yet, as we also noted, none of the differences have been observed in 100 percent of the gay study participants. In fact, in most of these studies there have been significant groups of gay respondents who don't have the trait, generally around 30 percent. This 30 percent of respondents, all self-identified as gay, tended to present with the same behavior or trait as the heterosexual male respondents.

What we wanted the survey to answer was this: Do gender differences come into play in the success or failure of long-term gay male relationships? As we have seen in earlier chapters, there is a biological basis, an organic reason that men and women exhibit differences in mating behaviors. Such differences are communicated in hundreds, if not thousands, of ways in our daily lives, in everything from our dress to our social policies. We all are affected by these subtle differences between men and women, but is this the key to a happy and successful long-term relationship between two gay men? In order to get a truly clear picture of the impact of these differences, it seemed important to gather information on the real lives of gay men, to ask straight out: What turns you on, what do you look for in a mate, what is sexy, and what is a turnoff?

MEASURING MATING STRATEGIES

How does one measure something that seems so organic, so natural, yet so undefined, as love? Devising a survey to test for love, per se, is nearly impossible—but a test of *specific gender mating traits* isn't. Human desire, as reflected by mating behaviors, attitudes, and specific traits, is obviously central to successful mating and, as such, is measurable. While it may be hard to ask someone to quantify love, asking him what hair color he finds attractive is another thing.

In heterosexual men, as we have seen, the essential desired characteristics of a mate are fairly simple: youthfulness, fertility, and bilateral physical symmetry in the face and body. In addition, certain physical characteristics, such as larger breasts, are considered desirable traits. Heterosexual women find desirable in a mate: status, resources, intelligence, and bilateral physical symmetry, again with specific physical traits, such as broad shoulders.

One way to build a survey that would give us greater insight into the evolutionary tinkering inside the heads of gay men when seeking mates was to create a list of specific indicators of gender-specific mating traits. In other words, in order to better understand what makes a successful gay relationship, we

"Freezing my balls off..." David said when I asked him if he needed a ride. I took that as a yes and pushed the passenger door open. A quick jolt surged through me when he said the word "balls." David was the type of guy who'd been my weakness when I was in high school: a little rough around the edges, but kind inside. He was muscular, had sun-blond hair, and was always in need of a shave, even though he was only in tenth grade. No matter what shirt he wore, the brown hair on his chest could be seen peeking over the top. I stole his T-shirt from gym class once and used it to masturbate with for weeks afterwards. I really wanted his jock strap, but couldn't come up with an excuse for that, whereas it would have been easy to simply say I needed to borrow his T-shirt if I had been caught stealing it.

It struck me at the time that David wasn't just masculine, but hyper-masculine. He had numerous indicators of masculinity: hairy chest, legs, ass. He had a

had to understand what physical and psychological traits gay men found attractive in other men. Once I had created a list of traits, I'd simply ask gay men to respond to what they found appealing and what they didn't. If nothing else, I'd certainly get some interesting answers to questions that no one had asked gay men before.

The resulting survey, known as the National Male Relationship Survey, or the NMRS, began with the obligatory gathering of basic demographic information, which was useful in determining how well our responding population correlated with the general population. Then the survey dove into the questions of sex and love and marriage and other, more subtle deep voice and a cocky manner. He could grin his way out of any situation. He was physically and emotionally strong. He was certainly masculine enough to not worry about what others said about him. Thus, he was able to not only be my friend, but to also put his arm across my shoulders, pulling me close, when I made him laugh.

He smoked cigarettes and worked on cars at an auto body shop. He even smelled masculine to me. Not like body odor, but manly. I learned later in an intro psych class that humans could smell gender differences easily. Women's hands smell different than men's. In one class we lined up with our eyes closed and smelled the hands of various classmates and tried to identify their gender. We were successful most of the time, yet oddly, my fellow students more often identified my hands as those of a woman than those of a man.

—*Tomas, 30*

mating strategies. With that in mind, I also had to devise a list of common male mating traits and contrasting female mating traits. Though no complete list of specific characteristics had been compiled, working from a variety of sources, it was easy to develop a list of the various mating traits men and women have used for millennia to find mates.

These traits fall mainly into four specific areas: the physical body, personality, mental skills, and social roles. Remember that mating traits work in two directions: there are the traits that you possess that draw mates to you, and then there are traits that you find attractive in others that draw you to them. Rarely do the twain meet, except when you're dealing with gay men.

THE NATIONAL SURVEY
OF MALE RELATIONSHIPS

Our 96-question online survey covered a wide variety of information, but was primarily intended to answer three questions:

- What mating strategies do gay men use to find and attract a lifelong partner?
- Do these traits fall into any specific groupings?
- If such subgroups do exist, are they a factor in successful long-term relationships?

People are always surprised to find out I am gay. Don't know why, but for some reason I guess I look just like Mr. America or something. I am in the army and love it. I am writing to you, per your request to answer questions, from Iraq. I have always been very masculine, never found myself wanting to be a girl or anything. I like other guys who are "real men" as well, but after our talk about differences in gay men, I would have to agree: I am drawn to "Beta" boys much more than I am to another Alpha dog like me. Sexually, I like to top and get at it quickly. Once I had a boyfriend who complained that I didn't like him after I was done. It wasn't that I didn't like him, I was just exhausted. I used to tell him to stop acting like a girl. He always wanted to cuddle. I wanted to sleep. We worked it out—I'd nap on my back and he'd lie on my chest and play with the hair there. It was nice. (I should look him up again—maybe I was too quick to jump out...)

—*Brad, 35*

The NSMR was open to any man, and was promoted through a variety of Internet sites, primarily Connexion.com (a gay political and social networking site) and Craigslist. org (an online classified advertising company). A target of 1,200 responses was set as being large enough to be reflective of the gay community, yet small enough to manage via data analysis. By the end of the first week, 1,203 gay, bisexual, and heterosexual men and 360 gay couples had voluntarily taken the survey. Later, I would conduct additional online and face-to-face interviews with other couples and individuals, asking more detailed questions, resulting in over 2,000 total respondents.

The respondents were men from all walks of life, of all ages, and according to their responses, were of eleven different sexual orientations and identifications. They were from four continents (North America, South America, Europe, and Asia), twenty-six countries, and all fifty states, thanks to the Internet.

I had hoped to create an accurate survey that would offer the greatest insight into gender-specific mating traits. For example, I always asked respondents to list their current profession, with the intent that later these responses could be sorted according to gender dominance in that specific career field. This way, I could see whether there were patterns in the employment choices of gay men, in particular, whether there was a preponderance of gay men in traditionally female jobs, such as ballet dancer, versus those who chose traditional male jobs, such as construction worker. The rest of the survey looked at everything from marital status, now and in the past, to the most intimate questions of sexual positions and preferences.

I drew questions from the four main areas of mating style and gender: body appearance, mental skills, personality, and preferred traits in potential mates. Many of the questions may

People have always known I was gay—I don't seem to be able to hide it. I remember one time my car broke down next to the road and I had to call a mechanic. Well, first off, the receptionist kept calling me "ma'am." Then when the tow-truck guy came, he was very nice and all, but as we were riding back to the service station, he turned to me as I chatted away and he looked at me and smiled and said, "When you talk, butterflies come out of your mouth, don't they?" We had a good laugh about that.

—*Drew, 40*

have seemed, to the respondent, to be from left field, but had direct implications for the answers about gender differences.

Let me give you an example of one such left-field question. Respondents were asked if, when they clasped their hands together, the right or the left thumb rested naturally on top. Thumb placement is an indicator of hemispheric dominance in the brain, with men more likely to be left brain–dominant. Since the neural system is reversed in the body, with the right side of the brain controlling the left side of the body, a left hemispheric dominance would result in the right thumb being on top.

Such information would be, in and of itself, interesting and helpful, but even greater information could be gleaned from matched responses in couples. If couples with the same thumb placement rated themselves as being significantly happier than those couples with opposite thumb placement, we'd truly have some unique insight. If we began to see an overall pattern, if we saw such specific traits that happy couples displayed, we'd be on to something not only helpful but important as well.

But there was a much bigger-picture question as well. Would we see specific groupings of men with unique clusters of mating traits? I think everyone, from individual gay men to other professionals in the field, assumes that while some of us are more feminine and some more masculine, underneath we all want the same things out of relationships and we go about finding and keeping a partner in the same way. Boy, were we wrong.

CHAPTER 5

Inside the Minds of Those Uniquely Gifted: The Survey Results

No one cares what gay men have to say—even ourselves. It is amazing to me how often I hear people who know nothing about being gay, but who are quick to tell you what they think about gay men, or to explain gay men, or whatever. Too often, these folks are just plain wrong. But that doesn't stop them from talking. And it really doesn't stop people from listening to them. I just wish some of these politicians or community moral activists would ask just one gay person what they wanted or needed. That'd be a change.

—Jeffery, 23

Q: Describe your sex life using a Batman Begins quote.

A: "Wait. You could die. At least tell me your name!"

Superherohype.com

SO, DID WE FIND EVIDENCE of our theoretical Alpha and Beta groups? And if so, did it matter to gay relationships? Two things had to be determined if we were to be able to say yes to both these questions.

First, we'd have to see specific clusters of men based on specific traits. In other words, Did we see specific mating-strategy groups, and did these groups differ based on male and female mating strategies? If our respondents had been heterosexual men and women, we would easily see such a dividing line; would there be a similar dividing line when all the respondents were gay men?

Second, when we analyze the responses of the matched couples, would we see the same dividing line or would the couples' answers be more alike? What would we see when we looked at happy couples compared to all couples? Would length of time together make a difference?

Honestly, there are hundreds of questions we could seek answers to—even as I write, a pile of new questions waits. But for the purposes of this book, we focused our interests on relationships. And the respondents gave us a general picture of gay men that is amazing. Who knew, for example, that a majority of gay men, if given a choice, would choose to have sex with a fireman, but would not marry him, choosing to marry a schoolteacher instead? Before we go deeper into the analyses of the data, let's take a scenic bypass—a quick look at some of the more interesting data discovered when two thousand gay men talk privately—and then come back to the big questions.

RELATIONSHIPS

How many gay men are in relationships?

As you may suspect, there are not a lot of gay couples. Our results were consistent with the 1995 Partners National Survey of Lesbian & Gay Couples and to the number of same-sex male households reported in the U.S. Census in 2000: approximately 13 percent of the respondents were in relationships. In the same population of heterosexual men, the percentage who are married or have a live-in partner is over 70 percent.

Are gay relationships happy?

Of those respondents in gay marriages or marriage-like relationships, 26 percent reported being dissatisfied to some degree, 74 percent reported being "somewhat satisfied" or "extremely satisfied." In other studies conducted with heterosexual men, 18.2 percent reported being dissatisfied to some degree with their relationships, while 75 percent reported being "somewhat satisfied" or "extremely satisfied." So we see no significant differences in the level of satisfaction of heterosexual versus gay male relationships.

Are heterosexually married bisexual men happy?

A majority—62 percent—of the men in our survey in heterosexual marriages who reported being bisexual rated their relationships to women as being dissatisfying to a great degree, 28 percent said they were somewhat satisfied, and only 9 percent reported being extremely satisfied in their heterosexual marriages.

I can't help but wonder whether these "bisexual" men would be happier in an openly homosexual relationship? Apparently they are willing to pay a high price for the social comfort their heterosexual relationship brings, and this lends support to our argument that bisexual men are gay men in the wrong relationship.

How long do gay relationships last, on average?

Confirming the suspicion that gay relationships tend to be short-lived, a majority of responding couples, 68.6 percent, reported having been together less than five years; only 6 percent reported being together for twenty years or more. It appears that the majority of gay relationships ended between the fourth and fifth year. Our respondents also reported having an average of three "major" relationships in their past, with each relationship lasting an average of just under five years.

Where do gay men meet their mates?

The majority of the married gay men met their life partners via three means: the Internet (probably reflective of both the current times and the sampling population); bars or night-clubs; friends and family. Those men who were single reported meeting men most often via the Internet, followed by going to bars, mate-matching services, then sex clubs.

Are gay couples monogamous?

Of those men who were in partnerships, the majority (55 percent) were in monogamous relationships, followed by 16 percent who reported being in a limited open relationship in which some outside sexual activity was allowed on rare occasions with the full consent of both partners. Another 12 percent reported having three-way sexual encounters when both partners were included, and the remaining 17 percent reported no limits on outside sexual activity within the relationship. The most common answer for men who had been together for more than twenty years? Yes and no: they started out monogamous, then opened their relationships, and then closed them back up after a few years.

Do gay couples live together?

While a large majority of heterosexual couples (93 percent) share a home upon marriage, only 63 percent of these gay couples did. Why this is the case is open to speculation. Some possible explanations include a desire for independence or a greater need for privacy.

WHAT GAY MEN LOOK FOR IN A PARTNER

What do gay men seek in a sex partner? Is it the same for a marriage partner?

The most interesting finding in the general survey was that gay men, like heterosexual men, seek different things in a sexual versus a marriage partner. When gay men are seeking a sex partner, they look for three main things. First and foremost is a sexy body, followed distantly by a strong personality, and finally someone who "found me sexy." When asked about marriage partners, gay men consider a much wider range of information, including a preference for a "lively personality," "a receptiveness to me," "common interests," "kindness to animals and children," and "an ability to care for me emotionally and physically if I am unable to." A "sexy body" came in as No. 6.

What do gay men like to do in bed?

The largest number of gay men said they preferred to be the passive partner during anal sex. This was followed by a large number of men who preferred to top. Good thing. Second in overall preferences in sex acts was oral sex, followed by masturbation. The least popular sexual act? We were unable to determine that—there were literally hundreds of single answers, everything from clown sex to mudding to pirate sex.

What is the sexiest profession? Most marriageable?

According to the respondents, the *sexiest* professions and the most *marriageable* professions are different. Respondents listed the following professions as the sexiest, in order: fireman, professional athlete, doctor, construction worker, policeman, and erotic dancer. But who was the most desirable to marry? Teacher, doctor, fireman, professional athlete, and policeman.

How masculine does a man need to be for sex? For marriage?

While the largest proportion of men answered that a man needed to be "more masculine than feminine" to have sex with them (74.3 percent), there were plenty of men (25 percent) whose answers ranged from "very feminine" to "more feminine than masculine." When asked about marriage and masculinity, a large majority (63 percent) said any future partner must be either "masculine" or "highly masculine." But again, there was that 37 percent who would opt for men who are more feminine. (Note the near 70/30 split again in these results.)

LOVE AND DATING

Do gay men believe in "love at first sight"?

Yes, 64 percent do.

Ask out or wait to be asked?

Overall, gay men preferred to be asked out (82 percent), as opposed to doing the asking. (Now, how's that going to work? If everyone waits to be asked, no one gets to go out.)

What is the best way to meet someone?

Perhaps every gay man in America should start using what 86 percent of the respondents listed as the best method for getting a date: a smile.

What is the best way to pick up someone for sex?

The best way to let a guy know you want to have sex with him is to stare into his eyes, according to 78 percent of the respondents.

What I hate most about gay men is...

Bitchiness, according to over half of the respondents.

What I like best about gay men is...

A laid-back attitude about sex and easy access to sex was what over 60 percent of the respondents said.

What is the biggest challenge to a successful gay relationship?

Ironically, this is the same as the answer to the last question: "sex is too easy to get"! Though there were many other answers, over 60 percent of the respondents thought sex was too easy to get in the gay community. The fact that a majority of respondents gave the same answer for the last two questions indicates that at least some gay men are conflicted by such easy access to sex in our community.

While these responses give us some practical surface information, such as the best way to pick up someone, they don't tell us much about the functions of a successful long-term relationship. In order to find those details, we had to dig deeper into the data. What we found was, to say the least, surprising.

THE ALPHA/BETA DIFFERENCE

Even as we first set out on this journey, we had a deep suspicion that there was some reason for the differences between masculine and feminine gay men. Our hope for this survey was to find an answer to one of the biggest questions we had: Do gay men fall into two groups? And if so, are the characteristics of each group reflected in some way in the long-term success or failure of gay couples?

Using a group analysis process, the data indicated that, yes, the respondents did fall into two specific groups. While no individual fit either group exclusively, there were significant correlations that indicated a pattern. And if an individual had a certain specific trait, we could strongly predict that he would have a large number of other specific traits.

Here's an example: those men who reported having been called a "sissy" as a child were also very likely to have played with girls' toys as a child. Perhaps this connection is obvious, but some of the other characteristics that showed high positive or negative correlations are less obvious: men who reported having played with girls' toys as a child were also much more likely to report preferring being the receptive anal sex partner, a "bottom." Now that's interesting.

Our results clearly imply that there are two subgroups of gay men: a group that employs more traditional female mating behaviors and a group that employs more traditional male mating behaviors. I'll refer to them from here on as Alphas and Betas.

DIFFERENCES BETWEEN BETA MEN AND ALPHA MEN

So what were the general differences between the two groups? Comparing four main divisions of characteristics—physical traits, sexual behaviors, personality, and social experiences—men in the Beta group were distinctly different from men in the Alpha group.

Beta characteristics

Physically, three specific traits stood out for Beta men: a lack of second-digit-to-fourth-digit finger-length ratio difference (meaning their pointer fingers and their ring fingers tended to be the same length), a lack of hair loss as they age, and a tendency to enter puberty earlier than their peers.

Sexually, Beta men tended to enjoy being anally receptive, orally active, and to reach orgasm before their partners. Men in the Beta group were more likely to describe being the receptive partner in anal sex as being an "emotional" experience. When seeking a marriage partner, Beta men tended to select men who were more masculine and more aggressive and who had rugged faces. Additionally, Beta men preferred sexual and marriage partners who were physically larger in overall mass than they were, slightly older than they were, and taller than they were. Men in the Beta group also tended to find the natural scent of a man to be sexually appealing. Betas were much more likely to seek outside sex than were their Alpha partners, as Betas often used sex as a confirmation of their attractiveness and tended to see affairs as non-emotional fun more than as a threat to the relationship.

In mental skills, Beta men reported having poorer math and science skills, a lower ability for mental-rotation skills, and poorer ability at object-tracking skills. Beta men dealt with the same difficulties that women face when it comes to tracking moving objects and depth perception, resulting in a higher level of difficulty with parallel parking and sports that require kicking or hitting a moving object.

Beta men also tended to have a high ability to read emotional expressions on faces, and the majority of Beta men were right hemisphere–dominant. When giving directions, Beta men were more likely to reference landmarks. Beta men were more likely to carry a child on their left hip and more likely to use baby talk with children. Beta men often found the slightest noise irritating, and had a greater ability to find and locate missing objects.

Socially, Beta men as children experienced a high level of both childhood gender nonconformity and the associated harassment. As a result, the men in the Beta group were much more likely to report having been teased as a "sissy" as a child. Beta men preferred to bring about group consensus and were okay being dependent emotionally and financially. In arguments, Beta men tended to let go of grudges quickly and to be less socially conforming. Beta men tended to come out at a younger age than Alpha men, with most reporting being "obviously gay" as children.

Finally, on an emotional level, Beta men reported higher levels of passive-aggressive behaviors and, when angry, more likelihood of acting out emotionally, as opposed to physically. Beta men also reported a very high level of depression, body dysphoria, and eating disorders.

The implications were obvious: the Beta group was using a large battery of mating strategies that we see used by women, though overall, this group did not appear to act more feminine. In fact, on an individual level, we saw many Alpha men who were rated as more feminine than many Beta men. Perhaps a better description of the Beta male would be "boyish," "impish," or "social."

By far, the most common descriptive words for Beta males were "caring" and "helpful." Beta males tended toward caring and creative professions, such as artists, counselors, and nurses, and tended to be leaders in their social worlds. Other descriptions of Beta males included "affectionate," "candid," "caretaker," "susceptible to flattery," and "gentle."

Alpha characteristics

On the other hand, Alpha men showed a strong tendency to engage in traditional male mating strategies.

Sexually, Alpha men reported preferring to be the anally insertive partner in anal sex, but not necessarily exclusively. Many Alpha men also reported a desire to be the receptive partner, yet they described the experience as a "physical challenge and pleasurable experience," as opposed to the "highly emotional experience" reported by the Beta males. Alpha males, to put it bluntly, are more likely to say "Fuck me" than "I love you" during anal intercourse. In addition, Alpha men preferred to be orally passive, lying back and enjoying the attention of their partners.

For sex partners, Alphas preferred men who had "youthful faces," who were thinner, shorter, and younger, and who had less body hair than they did. Alpha men also found natural body scents less attractive and a sexual turnoff. Alphas were much less likely to have sex outside their primary relationship, but if they did, they were more likely to fall in love and leave their current partner.

Compared to the Beta male, when mental skills were considered, Alphas tended to be better at math and to have enjoyed the complex science and math classes in school, as opposed to the art and literature classes that Beta men excelled at. Alpha men were more likely to give specific mileage directions, to carry a child using their dominant hand, and to avoid baby talk as being "silly." A majority of Alpha men reported being left brain–dominant.

Physically, Alpha males generally displayed the classic male pattern of finger-length ratio, with the pointer finger being stubbier than the ring finger. Interestingly, Alpha men were also more likely to be bald or balding and to have penises that were average length or shorter. A higher percentage of Alpha men had cleft chins and square jaws. Alpha men tended to be taller and heavier than their Beta counterparts. Alpha men also report a later onset of puberty than Beta males.

Socially, in almost all aspects of their lives, Alpha men enjoyed being admired and respected and saw themselves as mentors and guides to those around them. Alphas tended to report having been teased much less as children and coming out publicly much later than Beta males. In social groups, Alphas preferred directing over consensus, preferred to be self-reliant, and tended to hold a grudge, but did not use gossip to get even. Alpha men were highly socially conforming and, therefore, got along with almost everyone, except those who insisted that they come out when they were not ready. The downside of being socially conforming was a need for social approval, often leading Alpha men to remain heterosexually married. These men were more likely to be described as "masculine" or "highly masculine" and tended to be leaders in the business world. Words used to describe Alphas were "ambitious," "discreet," "assertive," and "athletic." Above all, the Alpha male loved to be admired and respected.

Both Alphas and Betas felt jealousy, but Alphas became more jealous when a physical indiscretion occurred, whereas Betas found emotional indiscretions more threatening.

The Alpha/Beta difference in happy couples

It's obvious if we look around that there are both feminine men and masculine men in the gay community. What does this have to do with dating and mating success? More than you might think.

In order for us to fully comprehend what these differences mean, we had to see if they came into play in relationships. There were two possibilities for the effects of Alpha/Beta

> My greatest beef with straight people has always been this need to know "who's the wife and who's the husband?" Like it fucking matters.
>
> —*Brock, 39*

differences on gay relationships. In the majority of research into heterosexual marital happiness, the belief has been that the more a couple has in common with each other, the more likely it is that they will have a successful relationship. But does this concept apply to gay couples? Would we see Alphas mating with Alphas, and Betas mating with Betas? Or would we see that opposites attract?

Like most psychologists and counselors, I had always assumed that those couples with the most in common were the ones most likely to succeed. All my training had led me to believe this and had been the basis for most of my treatment of couples, both gay and straight. But the results of this study proved us wrong: birds of a feather may flock together, but they don't stay together very long—at least when it comes to gay male birds.

Looking at all couples who ranked their relationships as "somewhat satisfying" or "very satisfying," there were a small, yet significant number of Alpha/Beta couples. But interestingly, the longer a couple had been together, the greater the likelihood of their being an Alpha/Beta couple.

In fact, the likelihood increased significantly, so much so that *every couple* that had been together twenty years or longer was an Alpha Beta couple! In those couples who rated their relationships as highly contented and had been together the longest, we saw a unique phenomenon: a strong counterbalancing of their Alpha Beta scores. On our 100-point scale, those men who scored highly in the Alpha range had partners who scored almost the opposite on the Beta range, so that an Alpha's score of 80 would be balanced by his partner's Beta score of 20. These counterbalanced scores in the happy, long-term couples tended to fall within a ten-point range, plus or minus five points on either side. It seems pretty clear from this study that Alpha/Beta differences are key to a successful, long-term relationship.

Of all the couples that had been together less than five years, only 8 percent were Alpha Beta couples; the rest were matching couples, mostly Beta Beta couples. The implication, of course, is that their relationships are destined to be short-lived. I can't say for certain that these couples won't make it, but according to our data, only around 8 percent of all couples make it past twenty years. Is it a coincidence that this is the same percentage of Alpha Beta couples we see in our group of young couples?

But what about our other question: Did we see the same 70/30 split between our respondents? Did 70 percent of our men fall into the Beta category, while the remaining 30 percent fell into the Alpha group? Well, 68 percent of our respondents scored in the Beta range, while the remaining 32 percent fell within the Alpha range—close enough for me.

These two final and most interesting statistics of the survey, concerning the presence of counterbalanced couples and the 70/30 split, confirmed our theory. Not only were there differences among gay men, and not only did these traits fall into two fairly distinct groups of Alphas and Betas, but these differences came into play in the success or failure of long-term gay relationships.

Simply put: Beta + Alpha marriages last; others don't.

And not only do they last longer, the men in these pairings report a much greater level of satisfaction. Those couples who had been together for longer than twenty years, and who reported a high level of satisfaction, showed a clear difference in the Alpha/Beta spectrum. Further analysis indicated the existence of a "mateability" zone: an area in which couples had enough in common to maintain interest, yet enough difference to maintain the stimulus that the essential difference brings. Too much commonality, A + A or B + B, resulted in partnerships described as "boring." Too much difference, extreme A + extreme B, resulted in tumultuous relationships, relationships prone to cycles of breaking up and making up until they failed completely. We had discovered nothing less than the Alpha/Beta Key to unlocking success in gay male relationships.

Now that we've confirmed the discovery, how do we put the Alpha/Beta Key to work?

CHAPTER 6

Superhero or Sidekick? A Test

FROM PAGE 1 OF THIS BOOK, I have attempted to decipher the intricate workings of human relationships, from prehistoric times to today, to translate them into a unique, first-of-its-kind view of gay male relationships. What we have found so far certainly has interesting implications—the greatest, of course, being the impact on lifelong relationships. The Alpha/Beta Key gives us a new perspective on relationships and opens the door to a new way to create a healthy gay marriage. The first step to achieving that is to better understand your own personal mating style. Are you an Alpha or a Beta?

This chapter includes a 100-question test. The Alpha Beta Mating Style test (ABMS) was developed specifically for this book and is based on my research, as well as on hundreds of other sources. It's a simple true/false test designed to assess the four major components in mateability I've been mentioning: physical appearance, mental skills, sexual desires, and personality.

The intent of the test is twofold. First, to give you insight into your own mating style, including your physical appearance and your interior mating style. Second, to show you the shadow score of your ABMS score, an exact opposite of your score, a score that, according to our theory, will indicate the type of person who would be the best partner for you. You will find complete scoring instructions, as well as additional information on the implications of your score, at the end of this chapter.

Steve: You know, Sky High's lowered the bar for being a hero since I left.

Will Stronghold: Umm, Dad, they're not super-heroes.

Steve: Aww, that's nice of you, son, taking care of the sidekicks.

Will Stronghold: Dad, that's not the reason they're here.

(Will pauses for a second.)

Will Stronghold: Dad, this is a rhetorical question. Would you be all right if Sky High named me a sidekick?

Steve: Yeah, sure, I guess. Why?

Will Stronghold: Dad, I'm a sidekick.

Steve: Who's a what?

Will Stronghold: I'm a sidekick.

Steve: Who's a sidekick?

Will Stronghold: DAD, I'M A SIDEKICK!

—Sky High, 2005

It's important to understand that developing a paper-and-pencil test that will accurately measure all aspects of human mating is impossible. The ABMS is simply a test designed to rank specific mating traits that we know are significant in human mating. The test is designed to encourage you to consider the implications of such mating traits in your current and future relationships. As this test has not been used over an extended period of time, it's not necessarily a predictor of future success or failure of a new relationship. But having said that, I will add that it should provide a good indication of compatibility on the basis of the Alpha/Beta dynamic that we have seen play an important role in successful relationships.

This is not a test of sexual orientation. It is assumed that the people taking this test are gay, but anyone, regardless of sexual orientation, taking this test should be able to determine their physical mating appearance and emotional mating style. Though it has not been tested to a great degree on heterosexual men and women, those who have taken it do fall within the expected parameters (heterosexual men tend to fall within the a/A domain and heterosexual women fall within the b/B domain). The test questions have been presented in a gender-neutral manner as much as possible.

THE ALPHA/BETA MATING STYLE QUESTIONNAIRE (ABMS)

The ABMS test results in an Alpha/Beta score that falls between 0 and 100 points. Scoring is simple. Each question is a true-or-false question, with the total number of true answers indicating your overall Alpha/Beta score. Follow the scoring guidelines at the end of the test for a complete ABMS score.

Simply mark an X next to each statement that is TRUE about you.

PART ONE: PHYSICAL

1. In general, others would describe my face as more rugged than gentle.
2. I stand 6 feet or taller.
3. I have a heavier beard, and tend to have a strong five o'clock shadow.
4. I have a cleft in my chin.
5. I have a square jaw.
6. My face shape is square.
7. My pointer finger is shorter than my ring finger.
8. My penis is six inches or less when erect.
9. My shoulders are significantly wider than my hips.

10. My waist is the same width or wider than my hips.
11. My body is more stocky than willowy.
12. I tend to turn down the heat, preferring a cooler living environment.
13. I have a high forehead, or I am naturally bald or balding.
14. My hair on the crest of my head grows in a counter-clockwise direction.
15. I have a strong bony ridge over my eyes.
16. I prefer to wear my hair short, off my ears, and off my face.
17. When standing naturally, my shoulders are squared, not sloping.
18. Looking at my head and neck in profile, there is more of a right angle than a diagonal line between my chin and Adam's apple.
19. When I was young, my body was markedly more muscular than soft or thin.
20. People would describe the way I move, when walking, talking, or dancing, as highly masculine.
21. I have not had an eating disorder.
22. I am rarely surprised by how feminine I appear in candid photographs.
23. When being photographed, I rarely find that I have blinked at the wrong time.
24. I am generally happy with my body's appearance.
25. When I hear my voice on a recording, I hear a deep, masculine voice.

PART TWO: SEXUALITY

26. I prefer to be the insertive partner (top) to being the receptive partner (bottom) when having anal sex.

27. I prefer to be the receptive partner (getting) as opposed to being the active partner (giving) when having oral sex.
28. I went through puberty at about the same time as, or later than, my same-gendered peers.
29. I came out later than most gay men I know, or I have not come out yet.
30. When I tell others, most people are surprised to discover I prefer men to women.
31. If I could choose, I would tend to have sex with men who have smooth, youthful faces, instead of rugged, masculine faces.
32. In my lifetime, I have tended to have sex with people who are generally smaller in overall size than I am.
33. Most of my sex partners have been my height or shorter.
34. I tend to prefer sex partners who are younger than I am.
35. I prefer a partner who deodorizes their genitalia and armpits, at least with soap, as opposed to allowing a natural scent.
36. It is important to me that my sex partners be slim or of average weight.
37. When snuggling with a partner, my partner has tended to rest their head on my chest, rather than vice versa.
38. Though I like being asked for sex, I don't have any fear of asking for it, either.
39. I prefer the feeling of "enveloping" my partner, wrapping my body around theirs in an affectionate manner.
40. My first experience of insertive sex (vaginal or anal) was with a woman.
41. I am currently married to, or have been married or engaged to, a woman.
42. My partner tends to orgasm before me.
43. I would say I prefer sex partners who have less body hair than I do.

44. I prefer to age gracefully, instead of fighting aging with hair dye, makeup, or surgery.
45. I tend not to wear cologne, preferring to have a clean soap scent.
46. I wear very little jewelry.
47. If I do agree to be the receptive anal sex partner (bottom), it is a more physical experience than an emotional experience.
48. I find the idea of my swallowing semen to be unattractive, but am fine with my partner doing it.
49. I find it difficult to identify other gay men in public.
50. I think sex outside my partnership is more an emotional involvement than a simple sexual experience.

PART THREE: MENTAL SKILLS

51. I tend to be pretty good at higher math, such as algebra, calculus, and trigonometry.
52. I am good at chess.
53. As a child, I preferred to do something active like running, as opposed to sitting quietly and reading.
54. Instead of giving landmark references, I tend to give literal, specific directions, such as "go two blocks, then follow Elm Street for one mile."
55. When clasping my hands together, my right thumb rests naturally on top.
56. If I misplace an object, such as my keys, I usually cannot locate them simply by thinking about it. I have to physically go look for them.
57. When parallel parking, I tend to check behind me by looking over my shoulder and putting my arm on the back of the car seat instead of only using the mirrors.
58. I can easily hit a baseball with a bat when it is pitched to me.

59. I probably could not come up with over fifteen words that mean "green" in less than thirty seconds.

60. I am surprised sometimes to find out my partner is angry with me, as if for no reason.

61. I have difficulty sensing someone's emotional state by simply looking at their face.

62. I can separate business decisions from emotional decisions, such as having to fire someone.

63. When picking up a baby, I naturally use my dominant arm to hold them.

64. I'd rather be financially responsible for my family than be emotionally responsible.

65. I am very good at reading a map and I am hesitant to ask for help or directions from others.

66. As a young student, I would naturally carry my books against my hip, instead of across my chest, without thinking about it.

67. When I was young, and would cross my legs, I would rest my ankle on my knee naturally, without thinking about it.

68. When standing still, I naturally stand evenly on both feet, instead of resting predominantly on one hip and leg.

69. I enjoy playing and/or watching one or more of these aggressive team sports: football, rugby, or hockey.

70. I can explain the basic concepts of the combustion engine.

71. Chemistry, physics, and biology were my favorite classes in high school.

72. When hearing fairy tales as a child, I would imagine myself as the "Prince" in the story who saved the princess.

73. I tend to enjoy "action" movies.

74. I can easily imagine myself sleeping through the night in a house with a crying baby.

75. I have little interest in "pop culture" or keeping up with "what's hot."

PART FOUR: PERSONALITY

76. I generally find societal rules to be more valuable than burdensome because they help us avoid anarchy.
77. When I was in middle and high school, playing team sports was fun.
78. When I go to a workplace party where spouses are invited, I tend to hang out with the men as opposed to the women.
79. I usually do not have a pet name for my partner.
80. I rarely use baby talk when talking to children, animals, or people I love.
81. I rarely notice people whispering in movie theaters.
82. I'd rather lead by direction than by consensus.
83. I feel that showing a personal weakness makes me vulnerable to being taken advantage of.
84. I pride myself on my leadership skills.
85. It would be uncomfortable to be dependent on someone else for my financial well-being.
86. If there are two drivers, I prefer to be the one who drives.
87. I have never really had any interest in dressing as a woman, even for fun.
88. As a young child, I tended to have more boys as friends than girls.
89. I tend to prefer jobs in which I carry responsibility, such as a doctor, lawyer, or corporate president over a job where I assist someone who holds authority, such as personal assistant, counselor, or advisor.
90. I am more logical than emotional.
91. I would describe myself as aggressive.

92. In general, I did not play with "girl toys" when I was a child.
93. I was never told I "acted like a girl" when I was young.
94. I could easily go to sleep, even if my partner and I had not resolved a fight we were having.
95. When arguing, I tend to grow quiet when emotions grow hot.
96. I'd rather be alone than try to resolve an unhappy relationship.
97. I have been so mad that I have gotten physically violent toward another person.
98. I tend to see my position as being right.
99. I am comfortable directing others to do what I think is best.
100. Others would describe me as classically masculine.

SCORING

Step One: The number of questions marked "True" on questions 1–50 = _____

Step Two: Are 26 or more of questions 1–50 marked "True"? If they are, the first letter of your score is an "a." If not, the first letter of your score is a "b."

Step Three: The total number of all questions marked "True" = _____

Step Four: Are 51 or more of all questions marked "True"? If they are, the second letter of your score is an "A." If not, the second letter of your score is a "B."

My AB Mating Style (a or b /A or B) = _____ / _____

My Numeric Mating Number (total number of "True" answers) = _____

My Balancing Mate's shadow score = 100 – My numeric mating number = _____ , +/– 5

Do you need more scoring help? Here's an example. If you answered "true" to 21 of the questions in Parts 1 and 2 and then answered "true" to 12 questions in Parts 3 and 4, your score would look like this: b/B. Your body would be considered Beta in appearance, as fewer than 25 of the questions on the first half of the test were true. Therefore, your first letter score would be "b." Again, the total number of "true" answers indicates that you have a more Beta mating style, as reflected by less than 50 percent of the total questions being answered "true," therefore your second letter would be a "B." Your total number of "true" answers was 33.

WHAT YOUR SCORES MEAN

We can tell the following things about the theoretical person who took the test in the example. First, his body shows signs of being softer and gentler. His face probably is more youthful than rugged, and he probably isn't classically masculine in appearance. His mating style is also Beta, implying that he is more likely to be passively sexual, preferring to be the receptive partner, and probably has higher levels of nurturing skills. The perfect partner for the respondent would be someone who scored 67 points. This score allows for a clear difference between the two men, yet is close enough to allow for commonalities to exist between the partners.

The National Male Relationship Survey data indicated that those couples who were happiest and who were together the longest scored within 5 points of their partners' opposite score. Therefore, we predict that a good match for this respondent would be someone who scored between 62 and 72 points. Greater differences (a score beyond 72) or greater common-alities (a score less than 62) would result in a partnership that ignored the two basic tenets of a healthy relationship—too much alike or too different—and would probably result in a relationship with greater conflicts.

A Profile of the Alpha/Alpha Male

The Alpha/Alpha mating style is not commonly seen among gay men and occurs in probably less than 10 percent of the openly gay male population. The specific physical characteristics suggestive of an a/A gay male are the traditionally masculine facial features we associate with masculine men, and which are often featured in the drawings of superheroes. Such traits include a rugged appearance, strong jaw lines, a tendency to more body hair, and a high forehead or even a bald or balding hair pattern. Additionally, a/A men tend to be taller and larger, carrying a greater sense of mass, producing a stronger, more powerful appearance. Their hip-to-waist ratio (as young men; this changes as we age) tends to be 1 to 1, with their waists being as wide as their hips. Their hips and buttocks tend to be smaller, and their bodies, in general, display a greater V shape, with their shoulders as their most prominent feature, displaying stronger musculature in the upper body. The most marked feature of the a/A male is the strength of his jawline and chin, both indicators of a strong presence of androgens in utero. The presence of a cleft in the chin is highly indicative of the masculine face. In addition, most a/A males present with stubbier second digits, the "pointer" fingers, in relation to the fourth digit. This is particularly true in the non-dominant hand.

Regarding personality, a/A males have many of the traditional male mating cognitive skills and behaviors. They report being much better at left-brain skills such as higher math and scientific inquiry. They test better at cognitive manipulation of 3D objects, have a greater ability to use maps, and a lowered ability to access emotions in other's faces. They are much more likely to report the right thumb being on top when clasping their hands together, an indicator of left-brain dominance.

In mating characteristics, in general, a/A males are most comfortable with a partner who is younger. They report a greater emphasis on physical appearance of potential mates, with a strong desire for mates between the ages of puberty and approximately thirty-five years old. Though gay male relationships are biologically non-reproductive, these ages reflect the heterosexual pattern of desiring women who are in their prime reproductive age. As a/A men age, the difference between their age and the age of desired partners grows. In other words, when an a/A male is twenty-five, he tends to desire men between puberty and his age, a difference, at most, of ten years. When an a/A male is sixty, though, he still desires men between puberty and thirty-five. As such, the difference in the partners' ages can range from twenty-five years to forty-five years.

a/A males desire men who are in their physical prime, and tend to prefer men who are less masculine than they are. They tend to desire men with little body hair and who are shorter and smaller than they are. The majority of a/A men also report being the aggressor sexually, tending to be the top in anal sex (though not exclusively) and being the one who asks the other one out.

In other social behaviors, a/A men take great pride in being the "provider," often meeting great success in business. In relationships, they see themselves as mentors and guides for their younger partners. They tend not to be overly concerned with the earning potential of their partners, thus it is not unusual to see a/A men mated with men who are in non-income-reliant occupations, such as artist. a/A men are concerned with how they are perceived in the community, and their partners must reflect this power as well, thus you'll see many "trophy" partners on the arms of a/A men.

With almost all a/A males, the need for public approval is keen. They are the most likely of all mating styles to have been married to women before coming out. They are the most family-oriented, finding it essential to maintain good relationships with their families. a/A men tend to be social conformists, following the general rules and mores of their communities and families. They tend to form long-term relationships, though many find it hard to maintain those relationships as their partner ages. Not unlike their heterosexual brothers, many a/A men find themselves trading in an aging partner for a new "trophy."

As a teenager, the a/A male is most likely to present as either heterosexual or, possibly, asexual. Additionally, he is the most likely to have "passed" as straight and the most likely not to have come out or been "outed," or to come out only on a limited basis. Once he does come out, though, the a/A male tends to be a leader within the gay community.

On the negative side, the a/A man tends to believe he is infallible, seeing himself as right at all costs. He may feel that a mistake by a partner is a direct challenge to his authority. Though he would never show his reaction, he is highly suscep-tible to public criticism, and often feels that he's on the leading edge and waiting for the rest of the world to catch up to his thinking.

Sexually, the majority of a/A males tend to prefer to be in charge. Though many a/A males may try their hand at being the receiving partner in anal intercourse, they are most likely to prefer being the insertive partner.

By far the strongest psychological trait of an a/A male is his confidence. He is supremely confident and is happy to protect those around him whom he sees as weaker or in need. Batman epitomizes him: a superhero who is working to better the world and is happy to take on the role of guide, mentor, or protector. The a/A male reveals his weaknesses only to a few, well-chosen men, men whom he trusts beyond question. He is not without need for support, but does not like his weakness revealed or highlighted.

What an a/A male brings to a relationship is confidence, guidance, financial support, and a sense of direction. What he expects in return is loyalty, belief in and support for his values, and acknowledgment of his value in his partner's life. He will love a partner who says to him, "Thanks for the life you give me." His perfect mate would be an a/B male, a partner with a handsome, masculine, yet boyish appearance (the "a" component) and a balancing, supportive, and non-conflicting personality (the "B" component). He may also be open to a b/B partner, depending on how feminine the potential partner's body appears. In considering a b/B partner, an a/A male will take into consideration his own personal concerns about how others in his social circle would react to his having a more feminine-appearing partner. Many a/A males find the gentle and flirty nature of b/B mates to be highly desirable.

Men who challenge the a/A males, such as other a/A males and b/A males, would, in general, be a poor choice as a life mate for an ultra Alpha male. Men who have traditional male mating styles (represented by the uppercase "A" as the second letter in our code), as opposed to a masculine body type (represented by a lowercase "a" as the first letter in the code), are, by nature, competitive with other males. These dominant traits, which the a/A males and the b/A males value in their own personality, would prove problematic in others.

A Profile of the Beta/Beta Male

On the other end of the spectrum are those men who have both a softer physical appearance in their faces and bodies and a mating style more similar to what we traditionally see in women. b/B males are ultimately male, yet they display a "softened" physicality, in particular in the areas that are indicative of lower androgen levels in utero. Signs of this feminization include a softer jawline; a rounder face; a smaller, more pointed chin; and thin, long fingers indicative of a more feminine second-digit-to-fourth-digit ratio. There has also been research indicating other possible physical indicators of men who have a more feminized physicality, including more feminine walking gaits, vocal patterns, and hair growth patterns.

While there are plenty of men in this category who fit the highly feminine stereotypes commonly associated with gay men, b/B men have the most misunderstood and maligned mating style. In the current political environment, the b/B male is seen as undesirable by many in the gay community, a form of prejudice that has contributed to many men missing out on their potential mates. Those men who say, "If I wanted a woman, I would have dated a woman," fail to see the incredible power of a gentle man who offers his partner support, guidance, respect, and admiration, all in a nonthreatening manner—something most Alpha men find hard to do. While b/B men may seem too gentle to many, they are not necessarily feminine in behavior.

b/B men come out earlier than other gay mating types, primarily because of an early presence of gender-nonconforming behaviors. Because feminine behaviors often appear in these men when they are young boys, b/B males report the highest level of childhood harassment. Of all gay men, b/B men report the earliest onset of puberty, a pattern extremely similar to the timing of puberty in girls. Because of this early puberty and the obvious nature of their sexuality, many b/B males experience an early and active sex life, as well as, sadly, a higher level of sexual abuse by other boys and gay adults.

The b/B male is often assumed to be "acting" in a feminine manner. While their true nature *is* softer and slightly more feminine than most men, b/B males do not display the extreme feminine behaviors commonly seen in stereotypes. Some b/B males do, almost as an act of defiance, heighten their feminine behaviors, at times actively questioning social gender norms through drag performances, yet the majority are not extremely feminine in appearance or behavior.

The teenage years are also a time for heightened femininity for b/B and a/B males. A possible explanation may be an

"You wanna suck it?" Isaiah mouthed the words. I was baffled by what he meant. The back row of the algebra class was where the outsiders sat. The gay kid and four stupid thugs, thugs who were known for disrupting every class they were in, made up the back row. I couldn't focus on the teacher, as I spent the majority of my time waiting and worrying about what they had in store for me that day. How did I get here? I thought to myself. I looked back at the kid who was trying to get my attention from across the aisle.

He again mouthed the words, "You wanna suck it?" His buddy nodded towards his friend's crotch. I looked down and there hidden by the desk's top was his penis, erect, pulled from his open zipper. "Suck him, gay boy, suck his cock..." The taunts continued. At the time, I was unsure how they knew I was gay, how they knew I would be in the least bit interested, but now I know. I

evolutionary one. It is common to see a blooming of sexual behaviors in both males and females in the teenage years, and teenagers are notorious for their need and desire to display their newfound sexual powers. Few women can wear makeup designed to display sexuality as well as it is worn (or desired to be worn) by teenage girls.

The same is true with teenage boys, who happily display their heightened sexuality through a variety of means, not the least of which is the display of their physicality through athletic prowess. Thus, for young men who have an affectional orientation toward other men and a more feminized brain, it would be natural to display a heightened level of feminine sexuality. The inadvertent side effect of this higher level of sexuality is that often these displays of femininity are met with social looked different, I acted differently. I was someone with the "look" of someone gay.

That's why they could tell I wanted it. My hard cock straining against my jeans was another sure sign, and they could see that, too. He reached over, took my hand, and placed it on his cock. I drew back, hoping that I hadn't revealed my interest. Nevertheless, I was confused—I did want to touch it, to suck him off. Was he cool with the idea of hooking up? Or was it another trick. Or was it both?

I'd made the mistake of sucking him off after school, only to be forced to do it repeatedly under the threat of exposure. He even made me do his friends once. When I finally told him I wouldn't do it anymore, he made my life hell. Taunts of "fag" and "gay boy" followed me down the school's halls. How was it that I was the fag, when he was the one demanding it? He never needed it. I did.

—Jerome, 49

rejection. In an ironic twist, this can lead to an even higher level of feminine behaviors because the intuitive nature of these behaviors is that they are designed to make people like you. A girl who wants the attention of her male peers often heightens her overt sexuality in hopes of drawing the affection of boys. A similar situation for a young gay man would be, and is all too often, disastrous. Flirting with a straight boy often results in private sexual abuse or an all-too-public social rejection.

Alternately, as other b/B males move through the stages of adolescence and early adulthood, we see a completely different path taken: a rejection of innate behaviors, replaced by what becomes almost an obsession with all things masculine. These young men will practice for hours in front of the mirror trying to appear more masculine. Often this rejection of self translates into a rejection of other men who display any form of femininity and is the basis for what has become known as internalized homophobia. Actually, this term is a misnomer; internalized homophobia tends to be not a rejection or fear of same-gender sexuality but instead a discomfort with the expression of femininity in men. Perhaps, more accurately, we should call this phenomenon internalized misogyny.

As an adult, the well-adjusted b/B male tends to be neither highly feminine nor falsely masculine. He is, by nature, a more gentle man, with a strong ability to be supportive, emotional, forgiving, and nurturing. Even in later stages of life, the b/B male is obviously more boyish, eager to please and be loved.

Profiles of Men with Mixed Mating Styles

Native American cultures historically referred to gay men as having two spirits, both male and female. According to Wikipedia, the name "two-spirit" originated in Winnipeg, Canada, in 1990 during the third annual intertribal Native American/First Nations gay and lesbian conference. It is a literal translation of the Ojibwa phrase *niizh manidoowag*. Theoretically, within every person, there is a varying degree of balance between the masculine and the feminine.

In the Alpha/Beta design of gay male mating styles, in addition to the a/A male and the b/B male, we find two others: the a/B and b/A. These two styles are, in essence, living translations of the two-spirit concept, a balancing between the hard and the soft, the masculine and the feminine.

In men who possess the a/B profile, the physical body is classically masculine in appearance, while the personality displays a boyish mating style. In the b/A formula, the body may appear soft and unassuming, but within, the personality is more aggressive and dominating than the body appears. While the a/B profile is fairly common among gay men, the opposite (b/A) seems to occur more regularly among heterosexual men.

Perhaps it is not surprising that these discordant body/mating styles often lead to confusion among gay men when dating. It's easy to assume someone is an Alpha by his outward appearance, but with gay men it's just as likely that those men who appear to be Alphas are Betas on the inside. Hoping for an Alpha and finding a Beta can quickly lead to a disappointing relationship.

With almost half of the men interviewed reporting their characteristics, b/B males are by far the most common of the four gay mating styles. Another fourth of the respondents tested with a score of a/B, the third most common was a/A, and the b/A male profile among gay men was rare.

As mentioned before, both the body and the personality can be manipulated to a certain degree, but it appears that the internal workings of mating traits are almost impossible to override completely. As a result, many men who are born naturally as b/B males can change certain things, such as body mass, muscle definition, or facial structure, and move into the more accessible a/B mating style. Changing one's personality is more difficult, though many men attempt to by taking classes or seeking therapy to build their confidence and assertiveness. This difficulty in changing one's mating style makes sense if we think about sexual orientation as a series of mating traits. Sexual orientation is difficult, if not impossible, to change.

The marked mating traits of the a/B male feature a traditionally masculine body combined with the more boyish mating characteristics that are commonly associated with gay men. For the b/A male, we find the opposite: men who have more traditionally "soft" facial and body features, yet present with a stronger, masculine mating personality. Often the aggressive mating traits of these men override the first impressions of their boyish bodies and faces, and as a result, they come across as more masculine than they appear when they are not animated, such as when they are sleeping or in

I drove by the first gay bar I ever went to, probably ten times. I was eighteen and at a conference, my first real time away from home. I had come to present a paper on cognitive dissonance, that imbalanced feeling that occurs when we realize that we may have made a bad decision, but insist that our decision was the best, like when one spends money on a lemon of a car only to claim it's the greatest car they've ever owned, just so they don't look foolish to others.

On my tenth time by the bar I finally drew up the nerve to pull in, stop, and go in. The darkness was overwhelming, the smoke thick, the men undressed to varying degrees. As I nervously made my way to the bar at the far end of a hallway, I realized that I had to pass through a gauntlet of men so tight it was impossible to not brush up against them to simply get through. As I made my way through, my butt was pinched and groped more than once. I was thrilled and repulsed at the same time.

After I bought my first beer, I quickly was tutored in the mating behaviors of (these) gay men. I smiled and started chatting with another guy leaning against the bar. "Shut up" was all he said. Shocked, I started mimicking the expected behavior: lean against the wall, thumb in belt loop, don't smile. I stood there for a while until a guy approached.

He was exactly what I was looking for. Lane had dark eyes, a five o'clock shadow, stood taller than me, and was built like a Greek god. He wore a T-shirt with a Superman logo over the left breast. His chest hair curled up over the neckline.

"Hey, you want to go back to my place?" was all he said. It was all he had to say. I spent the next two days, not in the academic pursuit that I had come to Atlanta for, but in his bed. I was in love and never wanted to leave him. After all my years worrying that I would never find a real man in the gay world, here he was.

When I got home after that weekend, I moped and waited for the phone to ring, calling his number only to hear it ring and ring unanswered. After two weeks, I was convinced he had given me a fake number. I was heartbroken.

The following day, he called. I went back to Atlanta the next weekend. On Friday night, after another great sexual encounter, we headed into downtown Atlanta for a late-night burger. As we made our way through one of the shadier parts of town, a guy with a pipe attacked us. I was scared shitless. I can only imagine what Lane felt, because he took off screaming—yes, like a girl—leaving me there, alone, to lose my wallet, my leather jacket (a gift from my parents for graduation from high school), and above all, my dignity.

After that, Lane wouldn't take my calls. Honestly, I didn't want to see Lane again. All I could think was, "So much for that Superman tee…"

—Harvey, 50

Mark sat at the bus stop, alone. He wore a suit and tie, which seemed a contradiction when considering his amazingly youthful face. He was handsome and rugged, with dark hair and a five o'clock shadow at nine in the morning. He was the type of man who made both men and women turn and look. He had worked as a model before he became an IT guy, and I know it sounds like a cliché, but he looked like Clark Kent in his glasses. I was surprised when he caught my eye, smiling at me, not angry like I expected when he caught me looking.

Over the weeks, we struck up a conversation, and he became my obsession. Even though I didn't know he was gay, I was in love with him. After a night of drinking, we ended up back at his apartment, giving each other naked massages. He popped a woody, I followed his lead, we fell into his bed and fucked like men who had been on hold for too long. Afterward, Mark curled into my arms, resting his head on my chest, and slept like a puppy. It felt odd to me in some way, but he was so adorable.

Over the next year we tried to make it as a couple since we liked each other so much, but eventually he called it quits, telling me that kissing me was like kissing

photographs. Some b/A males may be described as having a "Napoleon complex," meaning they increase their assertiveness to overcome their perceived physical weaknesses.

This combination of differing physical appearance and mating style results in, for many, confusion when it comes to finding and keeping a partner. It is probably the primary conflict between men trying to couple. Choosing a mate based on physical appearance, especially one who is highly masculine, results in an assumption that the interior, the personality, will his sister. I was devastated. Not only was I losing this incredibly handsome man, but he was also insulting me in the process! Nevertheless, he was right. Even though we loved the sex we had together, there was something that kept us from kissing each other. Something was amiss.

It took months for me to get okay enough to even talk with Mark. It wasn't until five years later that I finally understood what had happened between us. We started dating again, and this time I used a different approach. I "Alpha-ed" him, being the strong, supportive partner, his protection against the dangerous outside world. He fell for me like a ton of bricks. I was miserable. My image of him began to fall apart and I felt too vulnerable, too exposed to those same dangers. Besides, I was pretending to be someone I wasn't. I realized that I had to break it off.

He took months to get over it, but eventually we grew to understand what happened. We loved each other, and still do. Like brothers (or sisters, perhaps...). Now we are both married to healthy men, who provide us a safe world in which we can live our lives fully.

—Denver, 32

be masculine as well. While the discovery of a gentle man inside a masculine body can be highly rewarding, some may be disappointed.

Of course, within every mating style, you will find a continuum of characteristics. While a/A men will universally display a strong jaw, there is still a degree of variation within the group. The same is probably even truer within the a/B group and the b/A groups. Within these groups, you will see men who display a slight variation in the two-digit-to-four-digit finger ratios, but it will not be as noticeable as it is in a/A males, or completely missing, as it is in b/B males.

The majority of men in these two groups would probably be described as "average" in appearance and behaviors, yet always to some degree, they seem slightly different from their heterosexual male peers. (I am always struck by how easy it is to tell which is which in identical twins when one is gay and the other is not.)

This is not to say that there are not obvious contradictory examples. One I recall was a client named John. He was strikingly handsome, with a classic Alpha body and face, yet was a big softie inside, desperately in need of someone to care for and to protect him on a deep emotional level. Though many have been fooled by his appearance, his Beta needs made it clear that another Beta personality would never be able to meet his needs. I should have known he was alpha/Beta when I realized how hard he worked to maintain his Alpha-appearing body and face through steroids, plastic surgery, and daily facials, a very Beta trait.

Extreme Scores

Earlier I said that there is not necessarily someone for everyone. What many people may find surprising is that extremes in mating traits tend to go unmatched. It is an odd human trait, yet, the more "average" a face is, the more attractive we find it. Those men who find themselves with scores on the far reaches of the test, scoring 91 or greater, or 9 or less, may find difficulty obtaining and/or keeping a life partner. Such extremes tend to be difficult to match simply because they are so rare.

The human species prefers to mate with people who are "average," not unique, because people who appear "average" are considered *normal*—that is, genetically healthy. The more common you are, the more likely you'll find another suitable mate. This is bad news for many men in the gay community who pride themselves on uniqueness. Yet the truth is that those men who see themselves as "one of a kind" tend to remain just that—"one" instead of "two."

Changing One's ABMS Score

I have often run into men who are uncomfortable with their scores and decide they will either change their physical appearance to look younger or attempt to masculinize their behaviors. There is certainly a social benefit to appearing more masculine in our current world, as masculine men are afforded more respect and are perceived to be more desirable mates. Even the majority of a/A's tend to be drawn to a/B's more than to b/B's. Research does indicate that manipulating these factors, such as changing facial features through plastic surgery, may actually increase the number of potential partners, but doing so often results in problems, as you saw with Denver's story.

One problem is that such changes are probably not going to accomplish your goal. For example, if you are a b/B attempting to increase your physical masculinity, you may see an increase in the number of men who find you *sexually attractive,* but your new suitors probably will not find you more *emotionally attractive*—the more important component in mating success.

Another problem is that increasing your physical or behavioral masculinity may backfire, drawing many more Betas than Alphas to you.

Finally, there is a misconception among many gay men that it "takes like to get like." In other words, it takes a great body to get someone with a great body. Plenty of Alpha and Beta men have great, masculine bodies. But Alpha men tend to have partners who are not as highly masculine, who are more boyish in their appearance. Bulging muscles and rugged jawlines don't attract an Alpha mate. What does? Kindness, confidence, and youthfulness.

Though it is rarer for an Alpha male to consider changing

Lois Lane: Come on!
Jimmy Olsen: Uh ... I'll wait here.
Lois Lane: Oh, for God sake! Don't be such a girl!
                                    —*Superman: Doomsday, 2007*

to become more Beta in appearance, it does happen. The most common cases I see are men who are aging. Since some Alpha men prefer the sexual company of younger men, often they feel the need to try to change their bodies so they can fit in with a younger crowd. This is unadvisable. Doing so reduces one's innate Alpha appeal. Beta men prefer partners who are natural men, not manufactured.

I can remember clearly one such case of an Alpha trying to be Beta. The man insisted on dying his hair jet black, including his mustache *and* pubic hair. Not only did the younger men he was attracted to find him less attractive, but he became a butt of their jokes. Once he stopped dyeing his hair, he was much more accepted by this group of young men.

Alpha/Beta, Beta/Alpha...whatever. While this information may be interesting, is it helpful? In the next part, just as the alchemist does, we will transform our leaden scientific information into relationship gold—an accessible, easy-to-use process for finding and keeping a life partner.

Part IV

IN WHICH WE PUT OUR
KNOWLEDGE TO WORK

On a cliff high above the city, our hero mixes the potion, following the directions exactly as prescribed by the witch at Xanther. As he dropped the last ingredient into the boiling stew, he noticed the gloom within began to lift.

CHAPTER 7

Wonder Twin Powers, Activate! The Alpha/Beta Key to Successful Mating

"Wonder Twin Powers, Activate!"

—The Wonder Twins, Zan and Jayna

WE HAVE DISCOVERED some unique things about gay men, not the least of which is that they have two different types of mating styles. Two biologically different types of gay men is not such a far-fetched idea, though, when you think about our everyday lives as gay men. Take a look at the personal ads: How often do you run into the terms top and bottom, bear and cub, daddy and son, or even superhero and sidekick? There seems to be something organic, almost natural, about such divisions, so much so that these roles have become a standard part of our superhero culture. Batman had Robin, Captain America had Bucky, the Green Lantern had Kato.

WHAT IS THE ALPHA/BETA KEY?

The Alpha/Beta Key is simply the essence of what our research has shown us: Gay men develop, biologically, to manifest one of two possible mating styles—one that is closer to traditional male development, known as an Alpha style, or the Beta style, which is closer to the style followed by heterosexual women. This mating style difference has a direct impact on the success or failure of long-term gay relationships. The differences are, in essence, the key to success. If a relationship is built on the foundation of an Alpha partner and a Beta partner, the chances for long-term success and happiness are much greater than if it is built on partnerships between two Alphas or two Betas. This is what I call the Alpha/Beta Key to unlocking success in gay relationships. Of course, this is far from the sole factor required for successful marriages, but we know that, without it, success is unlikely.

The success or failure of long-term relationships is not the only impact the Key has. In fact, the presence of these differences between Alpha and Beta men plays a significant part in a wide variety of characteristics in gay relationships—not only relationships between romantic partners but also relationships between members of the community at large, dictating a variety of behaviors that every gay man, either Alpha or Beta, experiences. Before we can proceed to the next chapter, where we really get down to work using the Key, we first must answer a few questions that the Alpha Beta Key immediately brings to the surface.

A/A COUPLES, B/B COUPLES

For those of you currently in relationships who have taken the ABMS and have had your partner take it as well, there are, of course, two possible outcomes: either a counterbalanced couple, with one of you scoring in the Alpha range and one of you scoring in the Beta range, or a non-counterbalanced couple, where both of you scored either in the Alpha range or in the Beta range.

For those couples who found themselves in a counterbalanced relationship, one composed of an Alpha and a Beta, great! You have a necessary component of long-term success. Later in the book, we'll look at the other two factors that are necessary for success (good common interests and strong common universal beliefs or values).

For those couples who find they are in a relationship that is not counterbalanced, a major question hangs in the air. Are these relationships hopeless? I certainly am not going to tell you that these relationships are doomed to fail, but I will say that these will be difficult relationships to maintain. If both of you are determined to stay together and make it work, it can. But be prepared to face many difficult struggles. These struggles will not be limited to fights between the two of you, but will include fights deep within yourself. Questions of extreme feelings, both boredom and anger, are common in non-counterbalanced relationships. Also, many men in these relationships find deep discomfort, almost a sense of ennui, and an inability to feel safe and settled. Needless to say, you must feel settled if a relationship is to survive for the long run. But if you're committed to making your relationship work, you will.

Our research indicates that there are maybe three Beta men for every Alpha man in the gay community. If a happy couple is composed of an Alpha and a Beta, you only need to do the math to see that we have a problem.

THE MISSING ALPHAS

The number of gay men available for dating in the United States is only around four million. While that number may seem high, if we now factor in the Alpha/Beta difference, it automatically drops to half—that is, if Alphas and Betas were evenly available. But there is something else at play here: the missing Alphas. With Betas outnumbering available Alphas almost three to one, this seems like good news for Alphas and bad news for Betas. But I suspect that there are other factors causing this imbalance. Nature tends to create symmetrically, and odds are good that in reality there are an equal number of Alphas to Betas. If true,

Locker rooms were dangerous places for some of us when we were growing up. Not because of any fear of sports, but because they were out-of-the-way places, places where hyper-masculine boys, high on testosterone and bravado, would display their manliness by demeaning others, usually physically. A pecking order of masculinity, unspoken, but known by all, was the law. Sadly, I was at the bottom of the pecking order.

The locker room at my high school was designed for trouble. It was off the beaten path, a completely separate building from the main school, in an area only traversed by boys on their way to and from gym class. Those overgrown boys we called the coaching staff had offices in the building, but, well, they weren't the people a gay kid would turn to for safety.

This pecking order was evoked at the oddest times, at times you wouldn't expect, which, of course, made it all that more effective. It was like a punishment slot machine. Sometimes you'd get off scot-free, while on other days, you were in for a full beating. I felt powerless against these boys, most twice my size. This is not to mention I just didn't seem to be wired for fighting back.

Their motives were varied, but I know today that they all were pushed by their biology. Some of my tormentors were black kids who had been put down by whites for so long that the opportunity to beat the shit out of a white kid was reason enough to do so. Others were white thugs, children of blue-collar workers, or "welfare-ians," all with a chip on their shoulders. These were boys looking to take down someone like me, a kid who could read and write, and could even speak without a Southern accent. In their minds, I was an arrogant Lord Fauntleroy, not that they would have had any idea who that was.

What would trigger an attack I never knew, but there were many. Looking back, the physical violence against me was shocking, though I hear it still happens today. Over various occasions, I had a front tooth knocked out, a cigarette burned into my chest, my wrist broken, and my clothes stolen. Once I was force-fed a jock strap, another time I was smeared with feces and urinated on. And, contrary to common gay folklore, no, I didn't enjoy it. As I found myself sitting on the tile floor of the locker room, so mad, trying unsuccessfully not to cry, I could have really used a hero.

There were two reasons I survived high school: my best friends. For reasons I still cannot explain, these two jocks separately took a liking to me. They became, in my mind, superheroes. They protected me from ridicule, protected me from physical attacks, protected me from my own hyper-nerdishness. They both taught me how to act "cool," even showing me how to roll up my sleeves appropriately and how to back up a car like a guy (look over your right shoulder, putting your hand on the back seat).

What did they get from me? Undying admiration. But was that really enough? They never asked for more, but deep inside me, I always felt they needed something else from me, or perhaps it was my need to give them something of me. Physical contact? A softening of their rough edges? My love? It was, and remains, so confusing.

—Marcus, 40

what this would indicate is that if there are four million dateable men in America, and two million are Betas and two million are Alphas, using the 70/30 split, there are around 857,000 Alpha men—highly desirable, highly masculine gay men—missing. There is no denying that in the "out" gay community, there do seem to be more Beta men than Alpha men. As almost any gay man can tell you, if you step into any gay bar, you'll almost always find more Betas than Alphas. Why?

Analyzing our data, three specific trends that directly affect the number of Alpha men *available* on the market become evident.

First, men who scored higher on Alpha traits tend to have come out much later, with many *never* coming out. Also, the number of Alpha gay men increased with the age of the respondents. Is it possible that as gay men age, they have increasingly more Alpha traits? Highly unlikely, simply because testosterone levels decrease as men age, creating more femininity in men as they age, not more masculinity.

Second, a majority of the Alpha respondents did not see themselves as fully gay. It was more common for Alpha men, even though they may have been involved in active relationships with men, to identify themselves as asexual (no sex with either gender), homo-affectional (no sex, but in love with men), heterosexual, bisexual, omnisexual (loving all people), or as having an undefined sexuality.

Third, Alpha males reported an amazingly high need for social conformity. To a much higher degree than the Beta males, Alpha males reported being married to a woman or having been married to a woman in the past, stating that it was important for them to do what was "expected of them." Alpha men also reported a high need to be seen as "part of the heterosexual community and part of a traditional family." They were also much more likely to say they felt no need to "follow the beat of their own drum."

Finally, Alpha males tended to put a strong emphasis on meeting the traditional mores of their larger communities, and reported a high level of discomfort with many of the mores and activities of the gay community. Few reported having taken part in gay pride activities, having visited a gay bar, or having attended a gay community event. Many of these men said they didn't take part in these events due to feelings of alienation and a dislike for the other participants. As one respondent said, "If it means prancing about in drag to be gay, I'm not. I see myself as a straight man who fools around with guys."

Whatever the cause, it does appear that there are a lower number of Alphas than Betas in open circulation in the gay community. The problems that result from this disparity not only have an impact on dating, but also have a wider community impact. In societies where there are fewer men than women, the competition for mates becomes highly exaggerated, with the women often resorting to a variety of unpleasant behaviors in their attempts to draw mates to them. In such unbalanced societies, the women tend to display many more sexual behaviors, to be more concerned about their physical appearance, and to engage in gossip and other disparaging tactics to devalue any woman they perceive to be a competitor. Not surprisingly, these are the same characteristics that many gay men complain about in other gay men.

So now, after all that, we have to deal not only with finding a decent gay man, but one who counterbalances our "type." Though it may seem more daunting than ever, the truth is this information is going to make it much easier for you to find and keep a great relationship.

OUR FINAL CONSIDERATION

Maybe Chad is right when it comes to classic superheroes. But for our *gay* superheroes and sidekicks, our research indicates it's more likely that gay men fall into four types, with two major categories

I realized a while back that there are really only three types of superheroes (and villains, I suppose): the god, the human, and the human that becomes a god. Every superhero fits into one of those categories and they are just as basic as they sound.
—*Chad Nevett, graphicontent.blogspot.com*

of men: Alphas and Betas, superheroes and sidekicks. Many gay men I talk with are hesitant to take on the title of sidekick, thinking it diminishes them somehow. Yet sidekicks hold an honored place in our literature. According to Wikipedia:

Sidekicks also frequently serve as an emotional connection, especially when the hero is depicted as detached and distant, traits which would normally generate difficulty in making the hero likable. The sidekick is often the confidant who knows the main character better than anyone else and gives a convincing reason to like the hero. Although Sherlock Holmes was admittedly a difficult man to know, the friendship of Dr. Watson convinces the reader that Holmes is a good person.

While many sidekicks are used for comic relief, there are other sidekicks who are less outrageous than the heroes they pledge themselves to, and comedy derived from the hero can often be amplified by the presence or reaction of the sidekick. Examples include Arthur, who is much more ordinary than the seemingly insane Tick; Sancho Panza is more rational than his master, Don Quixote.

I think what's uncomfortable for many gay men is a feeling of unease about being feminine. From my own experience, I would guess that the majority of men reading this book will have the same reaction: I'm an Alpha and I want an Alpha.

Those gay men who desire a more complete, human, and emotional experience in mating—to be in love—must consider both the physical and the emotional mating styles of their partners. And in order for this to work for gay men, we have to accept one basic, uncomfortable reality: mating is a sexual process, and thus requires a variation between mates. In gay men, that difference is the Alpha/Beta balance. Thus, for gay men to mate *successfully*, we must accept that some of us are more feminine than others, more Beta than Alpha, and that that difference is *beneficial to relationships*.

While men may be able to deal with some femininity in their partners, probably harder for them to come to grips with is the feminine within all of us. Every gay man is feminine to some degree—if on no other level than the fact that desiring sex with a man is feminine in and of itself. Kissing a man, lying down with a man, and allowing oneself to be taken by a man can all be considered feminine; these are certainly not experiences

---

I'll be honest: I don't care for feminine men. They turn me off. When I was in school, even though I was sucking cock like a fag, I wasn't one. There was always the one kid who was more girl than boy and I would befriend him just so I could get some action. I never thought of him as a friend, didn't want to be seen with him, even. But he was good for a BJ when I needed one. I've been married now twice—I just see myself as highly sexual. No, I don't have sex outside my marriage with other women, just men. They give me what my wife can't. I wouldn't say I'm ecstatic with my marriage, but hey, it works.

—*Andy, 36*

> I was dating this guy once who was a STUD! He looked, I am not kidding, like Clark Kent, tall, dark hair, curl in the front, glasses, everything. He was everything I looked for in a real man. Very straight-acting. Everything was going great until one night I came inside him, something I was trying not to do. I apologized profusely, but he seemed okay with it. Then he said IT. He looked at me in the dark, and softly said, "I like it. It's like I'm carrying a little bit of you around inside me." I thought I'd puke—he was such a QUEEN in that moment. I never saw him again after that.
>
> —Steve, 29

that a heterosexual man normally has in his life. To desire these things is well within the context of femininity. But for many gay men, thinking of themselves as feminine is taboo, primarily because we have been teased about being feminine too many times in our lives. But we may be sacrificing our future satisfaction in relationships by avoiding any sign of femininity.

On the other hand, no gay man is completely feminine. Gay men are equipped with both the feminine and the masculine in varying degrees. What is necessary for gay men to mate successfully is to know their degree of femininity versus their degree of masculinity and then to find a partner with a counterbalancing style. This is accomplished by using the ABMS score and the preferred partner's shadow score, a counterbalanced score for potential mates. The greater your degree of masculinity or femininity, the greater the degree of counterbalancing energy your partner will need to present. Thus, if your score falls deep within the Beta range—say, 20—your shadow partner will be a man who scores high in the Alpha range, an 80, plus or minus 5 points.

Here is where we stand now: we have seen a difference between men and women that also plays a role in gay mating. We have seen evidence of this difference in gay relationships and have given it a name: the Alpha/Beta Key. We have developed a test to determine mating style and the mating score of potential partners. And finally, we have considered the bigger implications of this information. There is nothing left for us to do now but put it to work.

CHAPTER 8

Outside the Bat Cave: Dating Skills Part I

ALL THE RESEARCH AND CONTEMPLATION we have gone through so far has brought us to this: a newfound way to find and keep lifelong love in your life. Those of you who are currently in a relationship can skip ahead to chapter 11. But for those who are single and looking, these next three chapters are for you. In this chapter, I'll introduce you to a new process for finding suitable men in the real world that will allow you to give up the gay bars, gay bathhouses, and gay want ads. Chapter 9 will equip you with the tools necessary to establish a relationship, including a powerful encounter method that you can use to connect with virtually any man you desire. Finally, in chapter 10, you'll be given very specific dos and don'ts to follow, based on your age and your mating style. These three chapters make up a new, unique, and powerful process for finding a perfect partner for you. If you follow these guidelines, by chapter 11, you'll be joining those men who have already found someone in learning how to prepare for a lifetime together.

Here I'm going to offer you a new approach to finding a life partner, a more *natural* method, one based on the amazing power of the Alpha/Beta Key. This process is so easy it will blow you away, but you must be willing to do all I recommend in order for it to work. And trust me, you won't be the first to be trying it. Many men have followed this same path, just unknowingly.

So take a deep breath, stand up straight, and forget *every-*

thing you have been told about gay dating. I want you to start fresh.

STARTING FRESH

During this beginning period, I want you to do three things. First, if you have been looking for guys via the Internet or gay bars or bathhouses, or any other gay place, for either sex or dating, stop. I'd prefer you not muddy the waters by continuing to have sex or dates while learning the new system.

Second, if you have not already done so, please take the ABMS test in chapter 6. This will tell you two important things: your own personal mating style and the shadow score for your future partner. Through the rest of this book I will give specific advice according to your mating style, so you need to be armed with that information.

I also want you to take note of your comfort level with your mating style. Did testing as a Beta insult you or worry you? If you tested as an Alpha, did that seem odd or uncomfortable? What did you think of your shadow score? Is this the type of man you normally date, or does the ABMS recommend that you date men you wouldn't normally choose? Take note of these feelings and ask yourself whether this discomfort might be what's keeping you single. Being comfortable with yourself and who you are certainly makes finding and keeping love a lot easier.

Finally, I want you to begin a process of self-assessment. I do believe there is someone for everyone who is mentally and physically healthy enough for an adult relationship. And this brings us to the first real task of this process: a self-assessment, and perhaps an assessment by a professional, if needed.

During this early period, get yourself a little notebook to take notes in. At some point during these first days, I want you to ask yourself this question: "Am I mentally and physically healthy enough to be married?" Then ask your best friend if he or she thinks you're mentally and physically healthy enough to be married.

Later, find someone who knows you, but who isn't a friend, and ask him or her: "Even though you don't know me very well, do you see any characteristics in my nature that you feel would make me unsuitable for marriage?"

Finally, ask someone who doesn't like you a slight variation of same question: "Even though you don't care for me much, do you think there is some reason I shouldn't marry?" If this makes you uncomfortable, take note of that, literally. I want you to write down everything these questions bring up for you. I also want you to write down everything these people tell you when you ask them your questions. You might be surprised by what they do, or do not, say.

Near the end of the first week, begin to think about this experience. Were the answers you received, from both yourself and others, consistent in referencing a certain aspect of your nature, such as "you need to bathe more" or "you're a little pushy"? If so, the next step is obvious: be sure to shower or bathe every day, or be more aware of your effect on others. But if the answer is less obvious, take a few days to think about what others said to you. Are there any themes in their answers? Do they focus more on your physical being or your personality? Do they seem surprised to be asked, hesitant to answer, or eager to help? These are all signs that they are more involved than you think, and are probably willing to give their advice and guidance if asked. And if you reassure them that you won't be hurt by what they have to say, they're likely to give you a good, honest assessment. Of course, your ego needs to be pretty tough to take what some people may say, so gird yourself beforehand!

If the answers you received were focused mainly on your personality, and were negative, it will be best for you to have a series of meetings with a professional counselor, someone who is well aware of the needs of gay men. I'd even advise that you start right off telling the counselor why you are calling: "I'm trying to determine if there is something about me that makes marriage unlikely for me." If you're uncomfortable with this process, remember this is no different from going to your doctor and asking if it's safe for you to start a diet or a new exercise program. It is essential that you begin to pull any self-judgment out of this process and just let be whatever is. Trying to change without admitting you need to change won't get you anywhere.

Don't move on until you have addressed all the questions that came up during this time. If specific questions need to be addressed, you must have at least begun to address these problems through counseling. You'll be wasting your time otherwise. But if your feedback indicated that there was no reason not to begin looking for true love, it's time to start. But you will be starting anew, dating in a different manner than you have probably ever attempted.

THE NEW SEARCH PROCESS

As I stated earlier, the first thing I ask you to do is forgo any of the traditional methods you have used in the past to find a life partner. I am asking you to avoid gay Web sites, gay bars, gay bathhouses, or any other gay place or thing. If you find it hard not to frequent these places, at least stop searching for a partner while you're there.

Instead, start looking for your future husband everywhere else. And I mean *everywhere*—from the grocery store to the tollbooth—where there are plenty of gay men living their lives, just as you do. Reading personal ads, you'll often see men seeking someone who's not part of the "gay scene," which honestly doesn't make sense to me: Who's going to see that ad unless he's part of the gay scene? During your search, we are going to step out of the gay scene and not look back. You're

I'm a forty-two-year-old gay man with a superhero fetish. Like a lot of fetishists my age, I assumed I was alone until the Internet came along. I've since met several times with like-minded guys for costumed roughhousing and bondage.

—Savage Love: "I Have a Superhero Fetish," by Dan Savage, Village Voice

about to open the door to hundreds of thousands of other men, one of whom is Mr. Right.

The process of dating and mating in the heterosexual community has been defined and redefined by social understandings, with evolutionary underpinnings, and with only slight modifications over time. And for heterosexual men, the system seems to be pretty successful. For gay men, though, the process of moving from single to married has been, at best, tenuous. But we're about to change all that for gay men, and start you using the same process that works for straight men.

Meeting someone, the first step in finding love, while it may sound simple, is often far from simple for most gay men. In the NMRS, more respondents reported having met their future partner via the Internet than any other means. Historically, more partnered men have met in gay bars. Both of these avenues have problems.

Gay men come from every walk of life, something that we have always prided ourselves on. But such diversity causes trouble when trying to find a mate in a crowd brought together simply by the fact of being gay. A key factor in the success of a relationship is commonality—not merely common interests, but actually being from a common background.

Heterosexuals tend to draw mates from their daily lives: their encounters in school, at work, and with friends. Such

"If anyone here can show just cause why Barry Allen and Iris West should not be wed, let him now speak or forever hold his peace!"
"Stop the wedding! Iris is marrying the wrong man!"
— "One Bridegroom Too Many," The Flash

crossed paths naturally limit potential mates to those of similar background, socioeconomic class, race, and religious beliefs.

But for gay men, the historic problem of being unsure of who might be gay leads us to search far and wide and across all socioeconomic strata for mates. In the past, the gay bar was the primary place for making connections, yet the gay bar is basically a club for men with one thing in common: a desire to have sex with other men. Internet Web sites have even less restrictive entrance requirements. It is easier to log on and disappear behind a screen name that reveals nothing about who you are than it is to show up, in person, at a gay bar. At least at a bar you can see how a person is dressed.

You can see why finding a good match in such a diverse pool would be difficult. This is why it's important for gay men to seek mates in a more natural setting, within their own familial and cultural backgrounds. What follows are a few basic guidelines to finding love in the real world.

GUIDELINES TO FINDING LOVE IN THE REAL WORLD

Guideline #1: Instead of assuming that gay men can only be found in certain places, assume that *gay men can be found anywhere and everywhere*. Search for them everywhere, every day, in every way.

Guideline #2: *Stop seeking sex when what you desire is love.* There is no shame in seeking a man for love—but being too obvious about your search for sex puts you into the lecher category. Too often gay men get distracted. When they're looking for love, they settle instead for sex—and usually so-so sex at that.

Guideline #3: *Give up the idea that you can tell when someone is gay; you can't.* I advise you to do the opposite: Assume every man you're drawn to is a potential partner. I'm not suggesting that you hit on every man you meet. I'm just saying don't give up before the subject is even broached.

Guideline #4: *Stop being embarrassed that you fall in love with men.* Like I said, there's no shame when we seek love. Even in the most conservative areas of the United States, there are more and more people who understand that being gay is simply an expression of one's genetic makeup. If you don't agree, you're behind the times and contributing to your own debasement. You don't need to carry around a sign saying, "I'm Gay." But openly reading this book when you go to Starbucks is a great start (and I'd really appreciate it, too!).

Guideline #5: *Use the natural powers of the Alpha/Beta Key.* Remember that Alphas seek mates in a different manner than Betas. By knowing these differences, you open the door to many more successful encounters. Know your mating type, know what type of partner you seek, and know how each approaches and communicates interest to the other. Betas tend to be more outgoing, often wearing their interest on their sleeves, while Alpha men tend to be more reserved. It's important for Alpha men to be open to the approach of Beta men, even if it goes against their nature. Too many Alpha men are oblivious to the advances of many a potential partner, simply because they don't realize what is going on. Alpha men also prefer to be friends first and see if things progress, whereas Beta men all too often want

I had a client who was interested in a young man he saw at the bus stop almost every day. Assuming he was straight, my client avoided moving beyond saying a quick "hello." One day he ran into the same young man at a gay fund-raising event, yet my client was so convinced that this guy was straight, that even in this gay environment, he assumed the young man was simply helping out a gay friend!

Eventually they did move beyond the "hello" stage, got to know each other, and began dating. The twist? After they began talking, it turned out that the young man also had assumed my client was straight, or as he told me later, "He just seemed too 'legitimate' to be gay."

—Dr. John, 35

to move right into a physical relationship—primarily because Beta men use sex as a way to confirm their partner's interest in them. Finally, Beta men have to remember that Alpha men are social conformers, and need a bit of discretion. Don't go too crazy around them, or you're likely to be going home alone.

Guideline #6: *Accept that you're going to have plenty of false starts.* There's no substitute for trial and error. Or for persistence, either. Keep trying and eventually you'll find the right guy.

TWO CASE EXAMPLES

Seeking a life partner in the bigger world is both exciting and challenging. I've been using this new method of finding a life mate with many of my clients, and have at times accompanied them out in the real world (known as *in vivo* therapy) to guide them through the process. I'd like to share with you the success stories of two of these clients.

Mark

Mark is in his late thirties, well educated, and works as a lecturer at the local college. Even though he spends most of his time in front of students, he's unbelievably shy. He's not handsome in a classic way, nor is he ugly. As we began his treatment plan, the first thing I did was recommend he begin working out and doing yoga. He needed some improvement in his posture and needed to carry himself with a stronger sense of confidence. On the ABMS, he tested as a strong Alpha, indicating that he would best be matched with a Beta. He was aware of his desire to date men younger than himself, but had gotten stuck on men who were very young, around eighteen years old. Though he found most of his dates through Internet ads, he couldn't understand why his encounters with these younger men rarely led to more than sex. Or why the men he was dating often asked him to lend them money.

As his treatment progressed, I had him stop responding to ads and agree to go out only with men he had met in a public location. I also recommended that he date men in their twenties and even their early thirties, something he had never done.

We began meeting at a coffee shop near his house, certainly not one that was known for being gay. On our first visit there, he found himself eyeing the younger staff members, all very attractive young men. As part of the process, I had my client hold a copy of the local gay paper under his arm when he ordered. When he returned to the table, I pointed out that the barista who had waited on him was using body language that indicated he was interested in my client. In particular, we discussed the way the barista had looked at my client: catching his eye, then looking away shyly. My client had been oblivious to this younger man's actions, having been distracted by the sexy bodies of the other baristas.

The next time my client was at the coffee shop, he made a

point to get the guy's name, to strike up a conversation with him, and to find out what his interests were. Over the next few visits, he learned that the young man was interested in foreign films, and my client told him about the foreign film series the college sponsored and asked if he might be interested in going. The barista was delighted, and the two of them agreed to meet at the school theater the next week to see a film they both were interested in. When my client returned to the table and told me what had happened, I asked how it felt to be going out on a date. He looked at me in disbelief—he'd just realized that he had arranged a date without even thinking about it—and then he became scared! But he didn't need to be. The young barista was just as excited to be going on a date with him, and when they did they hit it off, as if, as my client describes it, "we had known each other all our lives."

These two have been seeing each other now for over a year. Will they make it? I think so. They seem well matched and they certainly fit the profile of a happy couple.

William

The case of another client had a similar outcome, but with a twist. This client, a man in his early twenties, is a classic Beta, but unhappily so. He works at a local bookstore and when he came to me he was very unhappy about his manner and his appearance. He had had a troubled childhood and was convinced that he was just "too girly" to get the type of man he desired. In our first session, I asked him to describe what type of man he was searching for.

"He is taller than me, older than me, makes more money than I do [he laughs], and you know, just likes me for me. There is a man who comes into the bookstore all the time who is exactly what I am looking for, but he's married." I reminded him of one of the guidelines of the system—never assume anyone is straight—but he was convinced it was hopeless. "Besides," he said, "why would he want a big sissy like me?" We devised a plan for him to begin to consider more men as possibilities, and especially to begin to see the value he would bring to any relationship. His gentleness, his nurturing nature, and his love of life were all highly attractive traits.

The next time he was at work, the man we had discussed, the man of his dreams, walked in, and this time my client struck up a conversation about his reading preferences. Eventually the talk came back around to what my client was reading at the time: a gay romance book called *Wingmen*, by Ensign Case. (I remember because it's one of my favorites.) William, bless his heart, spoke right up and told him the details of what he was reading and, to his surprise, his customer said, "That sounds like an interesting read."

The next time my client and I met, he told me he was surprised the guy didn't just turn and run away from him. I asked William if, during this conversation with his customer, he'd been thinking about getting the guy into bed or simply sharing a book he loved. He looked at me surprised: "That's the first time I had ever crossed this guy's path without wanting to jump his bones!" We had a good laugh, but the point was clear: he had connected with his customer on a human level, a love level, not simply a sexual level.

Needless to say, the openness William expressed to his customer led to many more conversations, and eventually the customer came out to him. After more than two years of seeing each other at the bookstore, William finally built up the nerve to ask his friend out on their first official date after the customer had been separated from his wife for over a year.

Both of these stories have fairytale endings, but of course, not all individual encounters end happily. This is why keeping a long-range perspective is important. Even if William and his friend had not hit it off, if William had kept trying, eventually he would have found his happy ending. The moral: don't give up.

William's story does bring up the sticky subject of helping heterosexually married men come out. I'm not for breaking up happy marriages, but in our survey, men who identified themselves as being bisexual or heterosexual and having sex with other men rated themselves as less contented with their marriages to women than men who were in marriages to other men. Gay men, especially Alpha men, stay married to women for thousands of reasons, but one of the saddest is the fear many of them feel that they will never find true love in the gay world. Heterosexually married Alphas present a unique dilemma. One of the outstanding Alpha characteristics that Betas seek in a mate is a commitment to responsibilities, yet it is this very trait that often keeps Alpha males in their heterosexual marriages.

Seeking hidden Alphas "in the wild" is uncomfortable for many Beta men. This fear is unfounded, and is based on the false assumption on both sides that the gay man is only approaching the stranger for sex. The way to connect with any man, regardless of his sexuality, is by forming a friendship with him. Every time you meet someone who interests you, you must do three things: smile, introduce yourself, get (and remember!) his name. Never be needy when you approach someone. Instead, think that you have something he would benefit from. And I honestly think that in most cases, gay men who are married to straight women definitely benefit from ending those marriages and forming healthy gay relationships instead.

This subject leads into two more key points I want to make about seeking connections with men when you don't know whether they're gay or straight.

First, the vast majority of gay men I know are uncomfortable trying to establish close relationships with straight men. I strongly recommend that every gay man have at least one close straight male friend. By avoiding straight men, you lose a huge population of men in your lives, both as friends and as potential sources for partners. Establishing a friendship with a straight man is simple: be interested in him and what he enjoys. People like being liked. And once you've established that you like them, they're going to start liking you, even after you subtly come out to them.

When meeting a stranger, enter into a conversation with one intent: being friendly. By just being friendly, the worst that could come from establishing a connection with a straight man is that you make another friend. The best could be that he's the missing Alpha you've been looking for.

The second point I want to stress is that no gay man should ever put himself in a dangerous situation. Never sexually approach or flirt with men you don't know well. In addition, I would advise against any encounters where alcohol is involved. It messes up both your and your partner's judgment.

The process of meeting a man you find attractive in public is simple: take a deep breath, open your heart, turn to him, smile, introduce yourself, and ask his name. *And that's it.* Don't ask for anything other than his name. If he continues the conversation, great; if not, don't give up. You've opened the door. From this meeting forward, smile every time you see him and say hello. Remember, even if he scowls, you have nothing to be ashamed of: you were being friendly, not lecherous. You're only being lecherous if you want sex, and only sex, from him. You don't. You want to give him something very valuable: your interest, your friendship, and possibly your love. While you might find him sexually attractive, you have a higher goal than just sex. And even if he turns out to be straight, you've begun making a new friend. Don't forget that if he's nice enough for you to date and possibly marry, he's definitely nice enough to have as a friend. And who knows—maybe he has a nice friend to introduce you to.

As Guideline #6 indicates, you will experience plenty of false starts. But don't give up; there are plenty of gay men in the world. We have limited ourselves to believing that gay men are only to be found in gay bars and other gay-specific locations. As more and more men come out and are comfortable being themselves in the real world, the need for gay-specific "hunting grounds" becomes less important. In fact, in a recent article in the *Denver Post*, gay bars were listed as one of the Top 10 businesses likely to be obsolete within ten years.

For most gay men, the most efficient method for meeting new men is simply to follow the natural mating system as closely as possible. In other words, gay men must search for mates the way everyone else does: at the office, in bookstores, coffee shops, grocery stores, libraries, theaters, museums, and gyms. Open your eyes and your heart, smile, and say hello to everyone you meet, and be prepared for a new group of friends and that special someone.

If you do as I suggest, I promise that within a year you'll have met the man of your dreams. I'm serious! If you seek a lifelong love, you will find that man of yours in his world, in the real world. Happy gay couples are never made by sitting at home and waiting for someone to come. After all, even a superhero needs people to call out for him if they need him!

CHAPTER 9

The Superpower of Love: Dating Skills Part II

SO NOW YOU'RE OUT THERE, meeting lots of men, but finding a need for more information to succeed. Here are some additional tips on the manners of Alpha/Beta dating. The vast majority of couples I see who have succeeded in finding a life partner tell me it's as if they had known each other for years and had just gotten back together. And this may surprise you, but *never* has one of them told me he was unsure at first. How can that be? It sounds like they were just in lust, not love. Yes, they were—and that's good.

FIRST IMPRESSIONS

As much as gay men are hesitant to acknowledge it, our first impression of someone's physical appearance is key to a future relationship. Why? Because humans are amazingly well equipped to read and assess someone, both physically and emotionally, simply from a microsecond encounter. As Deborah Blum writes in *Psychology Today:* "How we make and read the fleeting split-second expressions that slip across our countenances thousands of times each day is crucial to our emotional health as individuals and to our survival as a species." She goes on to note:

> There's a distinct anatomical difference between real and feigned expressions—and in the biological effect they

produce in the creators of those expressions. We send and read signals with lightning-like speed and over great distances. A brow flash—the lift of the eyebrow common when greeting a friend—lasts only a sixth of a second. We can tell in a blink of a second if a stranger's face is registering surprise or pleasure—even if he or she is 150 feet away. Smiles are such an important part of communication that we see them far more clearly than any other expression. We can pick up a smile at 300 feet—the length of a football field.

Within the first few minutes of meeting, we can assess a wide variety of information about a person. For most gay men, upon first seeing a potential date's face we can generally determine whether they are Alpha or Beta, even from a still photo. This assessment is gauged primarily through three main facial features: jawline, head movement and position, and eye placement. Men with smaller or softer jawlines are generally Beta, whereas men with strong jaws are seen as more Alpha. Wide eye placement equals more Alpha, closer eyes equals more Beta. Head movement and position tell us if a man is more masculine or feminine.

In addition to our ability to assess a person's mating style, we can also sense much of his personality, his self-opinion, and his sexual appeal via posture, presentation, grooming, clothing, and jewelry. Men are extremely well equipped to assess the sexual potential of someone from a mere glance. That's why we find ourselves eyeing a guy standing as far away as a city block, saying, "He's hot," and being right. Even if it seems unfair, there is a legitimate basis for the unconscious process of assessment that occurs when we meet someone, and we are all wired to do it, even when we don't mean to be harsh.

It is simply a biological and evolutionary skill. Suppose I gave you a choice between two men to date. At thirty-five years old, Mr. A stands tall, has wide shoulders, and wears a nice business suit. On his right hand, he wears a simple gold class ring. He wears no cologne. His face is open and inquiring, his eyes widely placed. His teeth are so white they almost glow. His hair is dark, and his masculine, square jaw and cleft chin show a slight five o'clock shadow. Mr. A was previously married to a woman. They divorced, but are still friends. An attorney, he drives a brand-new Volvo sedan.

Next to him stands Mr. B, also thirty-five years old. He's shorter than Mr. A, and his shoulders are slightly slimmer than his hips. His right eye droops slightly. He wears earrings in both ears and a loose gold chain around his neck. The gold necklace seems to highlight the slight yellowing of his teeth. He enjoys good cologne and wears it liberally. His baby-soft, dull hair frames his slight face and slightly hides his ears; his undefined jawline and small, pointed chin show no sign of stubble. His skin looks almost shiny. He's dressed in an "Opie Taylor" striped T-shirt, tight-cut jeans, and red Converse high-tops. One arm is full of tattoos. Mr. B owns an older Volvo wagon, but doesn't drive it because he doesn't have a job and can't afford to fix it right now.

Which man would you choose to date?

The point isn't to pick the "right" one, but to highlight that every one of us uses external cues to assess someone as a potential mate, attaching meaning to everything. Does Mr. A's suit imply employment at a high level? Do the tattoos on Mr. B's arms imply a more liberal attitude? Do the cars they drive reflect their social status, their political attitudes, their financial wealth? Sorry, but the answer is always yes. And it's a good thing. As you dive into the process of finding potential dates, don't fret about being shallow. Fretting adds guilt to a simple, natural process designed to assure you the best mate possible. Too many gay men, having been victims of discrimination in their own lives, try not to do so. But when it comes to

I knew I didn't care for him. I know it sounds shallow, but I saw his picture online and thought, Ugh. But I couldn't put my finger on what it was about him that I didn't care for. He wasn't ugly, unemployed, or certifiably crazy. He looked really good on paper—he was a doctor, after all—but... no spark there for me. We went on to date for over a year, one dull date after another. I couldn't explain to my friends what I didn't like about him, I couldn't explain to myself, even. But it went nowhere fast. Another dating year down the drain. Is it true what my friends say, that I just want what I can't get?

—Rod, 29

mating, you're really fighting an uphill battle. Follow your gut and remember: no spark equals no future.

This unconscious ability to quickly assess potential partners has an interesting side effect in the gay community that you need to be aware of. Many gay men, in particular those with Beta mating style, attempt to manipulate their appearance to attract others, not unlike women in our society who try to look younger or sexier, even as they age. Modifying their appearances, either through exercise, clothing, or plastic surgery, Beta men generally try to appear more masculine. But here is where at least this part of the natural system gets screwed up. When men with Beta mating style try to appear as Alphas, they throw Alphas off, who, by their nature, are not drawn to other Alpha men. Instead, these masculinized Betas tend to draw more Betas to them, a problem when trying to find lifelong love.

On the other hand, I have also seen Alpha men who have been, either intentionally or unintentionally, "Beta-phied." There is plenty of pressure for gay men to conform to whatever norm the majority of the community sees as correct. As the Beta community tends to hold the power in our open gay community, there is a real sense of right and wrong when it comes to what one wears, sees, and thinks, and even in how we vote. Never has a community that professes to support diversity pushed for so much conformity. The sad side effect here is the loss of Alpha men and the values such men bring to our community.

Finally, many men may wonder if it isn't possible for Beta/Beta couples and Alpha/Alpha couples to connect. The answer is yes, and they may actually have really hot sex. But the future of these couples as successful life partners is highly unlikely. Remember, the question isn't "Can I have sex with him?" It's "Can I be married to him forever?"

This whole process of trying to be something other than our natural selves is both a damping of natural expression and a homogenization of true mating sexuality. Though there are many who feel an androgynous society is the ideal, there is little evidence to support androgyny as a prime way to find and keep a lifelong relationship. The best for both Betas and Alphas is to remember this: you have a good, natural manner about yourself that the person who is a good match for you will find extremely attractive. The more you mess with it, the greater your chances of never finding your perfect match.

PERFECT MATCHES

We saw in an earlier chapter that gay men have four possible combinations of physical and emotional mating styles: a/A, a/B, b/B, and b/A, the last of which is rare. Now that you are swimming in the deep end of the mate-seeking pool, it's important to remember not to be fooled by exterior appearances. As we discussed earlier, it is easy for us to quickly assess a potential life partner, but what about those cases where someone looks like an Alpha but is a Beta on the inside, or vice versa? Normally, this wouldn't be a problem, but gay men's heightened focus on the sexual often draws our eyes away from our instinct. If you find yourself saying something like "I don't care if he is a Beta, with a body like that I could love him forever," it's best that you stop and reassess.

We know there are certain combinations of men that work well in the long run, and some combinations that cause real problems for both partners. As you are out exploring potential partners, I want to caution you against falling into a mismatched relationship. While these relationships can start well, they tend to end after a few years.

Remember, the strongest connections occur between an a/A and a b/B. These are followed by good working relationships of the a/A + a/B couple, the b/A + a/B couple, and the b/B + b/A couple. Physical characteristics are always less important than emotional traits when looking at successful couples. While many gay men may be concerned about falling into "traditional role playing," most couples easily settle into a natural pattern of roles that feels comfortable to them. While the a/A + b/B couple at times may take on the appearance of a traditional marriage, with strongly designated roles, these couples tend not to find this a problem. And as in healthy relationships of all types, flexibility plays an important role as well.

MISMATCHES

Matches to look out for when you're dating are those that are too highly focused on the sexual, to the exclusion of any awareness of mating style. In my practice, I tend to see couples who are poorly matched either because of conflicting universal beliefs or, more commonly, a conflicting mating style. In other words, many of these couples were either a/A + a/A couples or b/B + b/B couples. When I gave these partners the Alpha/ Beta Mating Style test, they tended to score the same on mating style, indicating little counterbalancing effect in their relationships. So a/A + a/A couples tended to be aggressive competitors against each other, often fighting over who was the most sexually attractive or successful. The b/B + b/B couples, on the other hand, reported high levels of boredom, and often sought outside emotional and sexual stimuli.

Though it may be difficult to determine whether or not someone is an Alpha or a Beta early in the dating process, there will always be early signs of conflict. Once the relationship begins to get serious, conflicts become more obvious. Do not ignore these signs.

One client of mine comes to mind. He found himself in a situation that made no sense to him. On his first date with a guy he really liked, they wound up in an argument over who should pay the check. My client was insulted when his date tried to pay for dinner, assuming his date didn't think he was "man enough." His date, an Alpha, was insulted by his rejection of his offer to take care of the bill, which to him was simply a sign that he liked his date and wanted to take care of him. In truth, my client couldn't afford to pay for their dinner at the fancy restaurant his date had suggested, but in his attempt to overcome his own "femophobia," he ended up paying for them both, feeling put out, and not seeing the guy again. Too bad, since it seemed they liked each other.

If your intent is to form a long-term relationship, my advice is to consider mating style early in the relationship. It's also important to be aware of two other things when considering a potential dating partner: the importance of common universal beliefs and the importance of common interests. Fortunately, like heterosexuals who seek potential partners in the world at large, gay men who seek partners in the world at large will find that, by the mere fact that we tend to live and work with people who are like us, it's pretty easy to connect with people who share our universal beliefs and interests. Even so, it's important to keep these ideas in mind when dating.

COMMON UNIVERSAL BELIEFS

All couples need to associate and integrate with those with whom we agree on issues that are most important to us: religion, politics, marriage, family, race, environmental causes, social justice, culture, or any issue that you use to define yourself. To do so, of course, requires one to be comfortable with being gay in a non-gay environment. There has been no better time for gay men and women in the United States. With each gay person who comes out, a heterosexual person awakens to the fact that sexual and affectional orientations are beyond our control and not a choice.

By being open in your cultural and familial world, you allow yourself to encounter other gay men within that same world. Additionally, for Betas, by being out in your general world, you are more likely to encounter those "missing" Alphas, those men who are most comfortable in their familial worlds. Meeting a potential partner at church, in the grocery store, or at a local political fund-raiser increases the likelihood that you and your future partner will have universal beliefs in common.

Though it may seem romantic to think of you and your partner bridging the differences between two cultural worlds, that's not an easy thing to do. If, say, you were raised in the United States and were comfortable with women in the working world, it would be very difficult for you to be married to someone from a culture that felt that women should not be allowed to work outside the house. Such is the nature of universal beliefs: we feel that our beliefs should be held universally, especially by our life partners. We may accept that there are people who disagree with us in the world, but to live with someone who disagrees with us, on something so important to us on a daily basis, is generally cause for conflict.

Many gay men may argue that by being gay, we belong to a unique culture all our own. But doing so assumes that all

I was active in fighting the ban on gay organizations in the Saint Patrick's Day Parade in Boston years ago. My parents and grandparents moved to New York from Ireland before I was born, and I consider myself Irish through and through. I was single at the time and, at a meeting called by the local Democratic Party chair to discuss other neighborhood matters, I went to ask for support for the protest at the Saint Paddy Parade. I saw Michael sitting there being all quiet and I thought he was really cute, so I sat by him on purpose. After I spoke, Michael came up to me and told me he wanted to help. I didn't know if he was gay or not, but we went out for a beer afterwards and really hit it off. We've been together now for ten years, and come to think of it, I still don't know if I ever asked him if he's gay or not!

—John, 45

gay men are the same and that we hold the same universal ideals. The very idea runs counter to our community motto of diversity. While many gay men may well be Democratic, pro-choice, union supporters, we are just as likely to be Republican, pro-life, union busters. We are everywhere, after all.

COMMON INTERESTS

Along the same line as common universal beliefs, common interests are probably the easiest, and most commonly met, relationship need. For those gay men who live in larger cities, finding interest groups for gay men could not be easier. Simply by using the Internet and typing in the world "gay" and your interest, odds are you'll find a group in your area. For those who live in more rural areas, the Internet is still a great resource, at least for long-distance contact. If you do live in a rural part of the country, you might want to think of establishing a group for others with your interest. A bridge club in rural Kansas is more likely to draw another gay man than you might think.

MANIPULATING THE SYSTEM TO YOUR ADVANTAGE

What should you do if the search system just isn't working for you? Then it's time to take matters to the next level. For men I counsel who are having a tough time finding and connecting with men they truly like, I offer an alternative method, a process that my students have taken to calling the Swain Stalking Method. Though it sounds sinister, it's a simple way of using the socio-psychological concept called the "mere exposure effect" to your advantage.

The *mere exposure effect* of social psychology, simply stated, is that the more times one is exposed to an unknown stimulus, be it an unknown food, an abstract symbol, or a new person, the more one will grow to like the stimulus. Theoretically, if you see someone you like but don't know, the more times you cross paths, accidentally but consistently, the more likely he will be to grow to like you.

In real life, it often works like this: in a new work environment, where you are exposed to people you may not know but see on a regular basis, you will sense a growing fondness among yourselves, simply from seeing one another every day. The social psychological researcher N. Steinberg noted a good example of this phenomenon when he reported the case of a young Taiwanese man who had written over 700 love letters to his girlfriend, urging her to marry him. His plan worked. After all the letters, his girlfriend did end up getting married. Sadly for him, though, she married the postman who delivered the letters!

There is an evolutionary explanation for this phenomenon, of course. It is human nature to consider anything unfamiliar as unsafe until it has been proven safe. The same is true even for other humans. We do not trust strangers. It isn't until after repeated exposure to someone that we begin to feel safe enough to establish a more open relationship.

So, to initiate the Swain Stalking Method, you simply need to arrange to cross paths with the person you're attracted to at surprising and unexpected places and times. These repeated meetings will foster the same feelings of attraction for you as they do when one meets naturally. To heighten the effect, you should combine the mere exposure effect with the arousal effect. This states that humans—in particular, males—will misread physical stimulus as sexual or emotional stimulus. If you were to combine these two ideas together, you'd arrange for your accidental meetings to occur in a place where the man you're interested in is physically stimulated, such as at the gym or during a sporting event. Doing so combines the mere exposure effect with the physical stimulus effect to create an atmosphere of highly charged interest between the two of you.

If the man you're interested in finds you the least bit attractive, such a combination of stimulation will probably be enough to push him over any hesitation he may have been feeling. A word of caution, though: don't push so hard that he takes a restraining order out on you! If your presence becomes uncomfortably noticeable to either of you, it's time to pull back.

AFTER THE FIRST DATE

However the two of you met and agreed to a first date, now that the ice has been broken and things went well, great! Now what? The most common question I hear after a first date is, how long should I wait before I call? The answer is that you should call whenever you feel like it. If you liked the guy and he liked you, there should be no problem calling him every thirty seconds if you want to. Love, remember, is a giddy chemical experience—don't waste it by trying to ignore it or manage it.

Too many men are afraid that if they reveal their feelings for someone, they may frighten him away. But now isn't the time to hide your true self. If you're the type to get excited and want to call and let him know you had a great time, you should. If he is the right one, he'll appreciate your enthusiasm. If he doesn't like you calling, he doesn't like you—and that's good to know before you go any further. With an ongoing good connection, the time after a successful first date tends to blur together into a whirlwind of good experiences.

WHEN THE FIRST DATE GOES BADLY

As hard as it is to hear this, a bad first date is good news. Good news in the sense that you quickly realized that this guy just wasn't right for you or that you were not right for him. The most common time-wasting thing gay men do when dating is failing to trust their gut.

As I mentioned above, first impressions are amazingly accurate and powerful. I often hear men in my practice say something like, "I wasn't sexually attracted to him, but I thought I had better give it a second (or third or fourth) chance to make sure." Don't bother! Remember, if there is no initial spark, there is no future. I know that sounds really strong, but I have never seen a couple who've made it who said they *were not* interested in each other in the beginning. Human nature has a system designed to go from sexual interest, to love, to long-term companionship. And you can't have a complete relationship without a sexual component. Is sex everything? Of course not. But it is one important aspect of a mature marriage.

WRITE THE PERFECT PERSONAL AD FOR BETAS AND FOR ALPHAS

Though I'm not a fan of personal ads, if you really want to try your hand again at meeting someone through a personal ad after giving my method a serious try, give the following ideas some thought.

The No. 1 problem I see with most personal ads is that they appear to be too much like employment ads, complete with a list of obligations for the respondent to meet: "I am seeking ____." You fill in the blank. Most men are not too keen on trying to pass a test, especially for someone they don't even know yet. Besides, the vast majority of the "prerequisites" that people are asking for are pointless. Honestly, how many people select a life partner based on penis size?

It has been my experience that the more successful ads work in the reverse manner. Those ads that "give before asking" are much easier to respond to. This is true for men seeking Beta males as well as those seeking Alpha males. But there are specific characteristics that should be highlighted according to your mating style and the mating style you are seeking.

Alpha seeking Beta

If you are an Alpha male seeking a partner for a long-term relationship, when composing a personal ad, keep in mind the characteristics that are appealing to Beta males: to be cared for, to be appreciated, to be provided for, to be protected, and to be admired. In writing a personal ad seeking a masculine, yet gentle Beta male, it is important not to put in obligations or expectations, as this turns off most men. "Seeking a smart, good-looking guy" immediately puts people on the defensive. Everyone wants to think they are smart and good-looking, but deep inside they may be afraid they are not.

No one needs that kind of test, right off the bat. Plus, beauty and intelligence are both often seen in the eye of the beholder. Along those lines, for Alphas seeking Betas, a face photo is helpful, but body photos or descriptions are unnecessary, as Betas are less interested in perfect bodies than they are in safe, nonjudgmental personalities. Beta men are essentially seeking security, so Alpha men who stress their ability to provide for themselves and others, both emotionally and financially, will foster a good response from Beta men. At the same time, showing personal weakness and laughing at oneself are also very appealing.

Key words (and their variations) to consider using when writing an "Alpha seeking Beta" ad are: "big," "safe," "warm," "kind," "protective," "understanding," "family," "home," "provider," "nice," "romantic," and "caretaker." Images to invoke in your ad include any safe, romantic, and masculine environment that you provide the reader, such as a warm bed in a rustic cabin with a roaring fire, complete with crisp white sheets and a down comforter, or situations in which you provide adventure or access to places the reader couldn't normally access without your power, such as, "Let me show you the view from my penthouse office." Stressing the reader's special place in your future life together is also very appealing: "My friends will love you for getting me out of the house once in a while!" An effective personal ad for an Alpha-seeking Beta would go something like this:

Hard-working guy in need of that special someone to help him manage his (at times) chaotic life—I can't seem to keep myself fed or get to bed on time! I bore myself and need someone to add a spark to my life. (lol) In exchange, I can offer a pair of big arms to hold you through the night and a mind full of romantic adventures that only two men in love can pull off. I'm into kids, dogs, and taking care of those I love. As for you, surprise me. I'm not expecting perfection. The only thing I ask is that you be a nice guy who can find a place in his heart for me.

You may note that this ad contains many Beta triggers: "hard-working guy" implies a good provider; "special someone" implies he understands the Beta's uniqueness; "big arms to hold you through the night" imply protection; "romantic adventures" shows the Alpha's gentle side; and "into kids, dogs, and taking care of those I love" shows his caring and protective nature. In closing the ad, the writer stresses his openness to a variety of types of men, thus reducing the reader's feeling that he has to meet some requirements or pass a test. The writer, again, restates his desire to be loved, something Betas excel at.

Beta seeking Alpha

"Beta seeking Alpha" ads are completely different in nature. While the "Alpha seeking Beta" ad stresses seeking someone who is able to care for the writer's "inner/home" world, the "Beta seeking Alpha" ad instead focuses on seeking someone who can provide his skills in dealing with the "outer/real world."

For a "Beta seeking Alpha" ad, keep in mind the characteristics that are appealing to Alpha males. Alphas desire respect, to be understood and admired for their unique position and challenges in life, and to be appreciated for their desire to be both provider and protector. Alphas enjoy being mentors and guides to life's problems, and love to help others.

As most Alphas are stimulated visually, be sure to put a photo in your ad. If you have a good body, highlight that, yet avoid highly sexual photos. No Alpha wants to see pictures of his future husband's penis or buttocks making their way around the Internet. If your body isn't exceptional, use a good face shot.

Forget the leather and lumberjack outfits (unless that's what you do for a living). Alphas are notorious for following social norms. Believe it or not, the more "common-looking" you are, the greater your chances of finding a match. In your pictures, keep your hair short and boyish, wear everyday clothes, and avoid any signs of too much "uniqueness," such as jewelry or drag. Alphas prefer men who are younger than they are, so you should assume you'll be getting responses from men older than you, no matter what your age.

It's not important to appear hypermasculine, just nice. While Betas may be seeking highly masculine men, Alphas are not. Alphas do not want someone who will challenge their masculinity, but someone who will complement it. Think Robin to Batman. Alphas prefer men who are boyish in nature, men who are full of life and can make them laugh. The No. 1 criterion Alpha men seek is a good sense of humor.

Key words (and their variations) to consider using in a "Beta seeking Alpha" ad are "lively," "funny," "sexy," "active," "smart," "admiring," "needing help," "open to advice," "seeking guidance," "home," "kind," "young," "youthful," "alive," "creative," "family," "compassionate," "forgiving," and "confident."

Here's a sample:

I know you're out there. You're the type of guy who takes his nephew to the baseball game and everyone thinks the kid is yours. You're a successful, together guy who knows what he wants from the world and out of life, and that includes a partner who can stand next to you, a complement in this all-American picture. You need a playful, sexy guy; one who is loyal, grateful, and adventuresome, someone who will help create a home that is full of life and laughter. That's me: a nice guy with a nice body and a serious desire to create a life together. I feel I know where I'm going in life, but sometimes it's all too much. I'm always open to guidance and sage advice from someone who's been there before me. I'm not interested in hundreds of men, I'm interested in just one: you. And I want to know more. Call me.

In this chapter we've looked at some of the ways that the Alpha/Beta Key impacts dating in general. But as we have learned, gay mating has a strong biological basis, which makes me wonder: as we age, and our bodies change, does our dating process change as well? What's an older gay guy got to do to find love?

CHAPTER 10

Even Superman Can't Turn Back Time, Jimmy: Dating Skills Part III

HERE IS THE HARSH REALITY: human mating is a young man's game. Luckily for us, love isn't. Now if we could just get gay men to realize this! Love and sex play different roles throughout our lives, and to have a healthy relationship, no matter how old you are, you need both, preferably from the same person. As much as we don't want it to, time does pass, and our bodies do age, and so we need to modify our mating styles slightly, as well. At eighteen, we may find a highly sexual partner to be *the* essential element of a relationship; at thirty-eight, we're more likely to be looking for someone with common interests and goals; and by the time we're sixty-eight, our goal may simply be companionship and commitment. Although mating needs vary according to mating style, as Alphas and Betas age these differences become less obvious.

The process of searching for a mate, regardless of age, requires a keen understanding of your needs, as well as an understanding of what the person you are seeking is looking for. Knowing these factors can save you from heartache and wasted efforts—and may open the door to a relationship you may have thought was impossible. Below you'll find a list of do's and don'ts for dating, according to both your age and your mating style. If you follow this advice, as well as the advice in the two previous chapters, you should be well on your way to successfully finding a lifelong relationship.

I am seventy years old, though I don't feel it. I am retired and have a very comfortable lifestyle. I am looking for a life partner. My problem is I only find young men attractive. Is it possible for me to form a healthy relationship with a kid who's still into video games and comic books while I enjoy fine wines and theater? I know it seems unlikely, but I don't want to have sex with an old man.

—Rob, 70

FOR MEN IN THEIR TEENS, AND THOSE WHO CARE FOR THEM

The natural search for a life mate begins with the onset of puberty, as the body begins its transformation from nonsexual child to sexually reproductive adult. Adolescence is that time in our lives in which hormones, so new to our bodies, can lead to a sexual experience with the slightest suggestion. During this period, we are primarily driven to seek sexual release much more than any emotional connection, though the two are often confused in this time of "puppy love."

Betas

The best dating advice I can offer young Betas is to take your time. For teen Betas, this is often a period of conflict. Because Betas' behaviors tend to reveal their sexual orientation, young Betas are often targeted for harassment, making social acceptance a high priority. The drive for social acceptance too often leads to sexual activity with other boys, or adult gay men. This, in turn, may lead to a pattern of confusing sex with love and acceptance, a confusion that many Betas carry into adulthood. I would encourage young Betas to wait, to be assured of a strong,

I started having sex with this very feminine kid while I was in high school. I remember being turned on at first, but once I had come, I didn't want anything to do with him. Kissing him was, as odd as it may seem, like kissing my sister. I was desperate for sex and friendship, and I was convinced that he was the only other gay person in the world. So I hooked up with him. I don't think he liked it any better than I did, but we stuck it out throughout high school. By the end, I grew to hate him, frankly. Since then, a number of relationships I have had all seem to mirror that one. It starts off with me "needing" someone in my life. I meet someone who looks hot and we have great sex right off the bat, but eventually it too becomes a "sisters" relationship. It almost always ends badly.

—*Greg, 27*

lasting emotional connection with any potential sex partners before engaging in sex.

Alphas

Young Alphas face a different set of problems. During their adolescence, Alphas tend to find themselves working very hard to maintain a confident and highly masculine appearance. It is not unusual for Alphas to be "the best little boy," excelling at sports and academics in high school. Yet, despite the happy exterior, many young Alphas find themselves deeply troubled, unsure of who they are. Many do not consider themselves gay, and are often surprised at the suggestion. Young Alphas rarely come out in high school. The average age of coming out for Alphas is twenty-five.

Alpha teens often wonder whether they might be gay and

When I was sixteen years old, I found myself head over heels in love with a very well known man in the community who was forty years older. Though I was convinced it was true love, one night when I told him I didn't want sex, I was shocked to see my "boyfriend" reach into his wallet and hand me a hundred-dollar bill. I was devastated. As a result, I have grown overly suspicious of anyone's advances. I am thirty now, but still don't have a boyfriend.

—*Alex, 30*

may experiment with both male and female sexual partners, yet often find these experiences confusing. Being able to perform sexually with a woman leads many Alphas to believe they may be straight, while the excitement they feel from any male/male experience is often written off to youthful experimentation, a high sex drive, or simply a mistake, as in "Boy, was I drunk last night…" My dating advice for young Alphas is the same I offered to Beta teens: wait until you're sure of a strong emotional tie with your future sex partner. If you have mixed feelings about being with another young man, you should explore these feelings in more depth with a counselor you can trust.

FOR MEN IN THEIR TWENTIES

When addressing the general heterosexual population, the developmental psychologist Erik Erikson saw the twenties as the decade of intimacy versus isolation. As mentioned above, however, this era for many gay men, instead of being a time for resolution of the intimacy question, becomes a late-blooming adolescence. As a result, too many gay men fail to resolve the question of intimacy in their development and continue through life growing more and more isolated.

Betas

The twenties for the Beta provides, often for the first time, access to a greater number of Alphas, but he will find that there is still a limited number available. During this phase of their lives, many Betas find a myriad of ways to connect with other gay

---

When I was first coming out, I was elated the first time I walked into a gay bar. There were hundreds of gay men, each more attractive than the last. I felt like a kid in a candy store; that was until I began to taste a few. Instead of treats, I felt like I had been tricked. This was in the eighties, and I remember the first time I heard the word "trick" and I thought, Boy, is that true. I had been tricked so many times it wasn't funny. Every time I thought I had found the right one, there was something wrong with him. Always something small, like, well, like he didn't love me. [He laughs.]

It always seemed to follow the same pattern. Once I had been through most of the guys in the bar, I joined in the crowd at the bar, sitting on a stool waiting for the "new meat" to arrive. We'd all have a go at him, and eventually he too would join us at the bar and become one of the vultures. Once in a while, though, a "real" guy would walk through the door, and for some reason, one of us would be chosen from the lineup, and they'd disappear from the scene, never to be heard of again—probably running some café or antique shop in the burbs. [Laughs again.] Sadly, I wasn't picked. I felt like an orphan with no chance of being adopted.

—Gary, 53

men, and under the false belief that gay men are all the same, begin to date other Betas, generally to unsatisfactory ends.

What my client Gary describes so well is the experience of many gay men, the Beta/Beta experience. These contacts tend to fail mainly due to the lack of an essential difference between the two men. While Betas may be highly available and very sexually attractive, the pairing of two Betas does not address the missing essential difference, the Alpha/Beta Key. The result is an unfulfilling relationship. This lack of Alpha partners presents the Beta male with a difficult situation, but since these are the most "mateable" years for Betas, it's important to rise to the challenge.

Alphas

For Alphas in their twenties, this tends to be a time of confusion and uncertainty. Many Alphas pass through a phase of "bisexuality," a period when they allow themselves to acknowledge an attraction to other men for the first time, eventually coming to terms with the fact that their sexual and affectional orientation is toward members of their own gender.

During this period of their lives, few Alphas seek a long-term relationship, instead opting for quick, often anonymous encounters unlikely to result in emotional commitments. Neither Alphas nor Betas find such arrangements satisfactory, but Alphas persist in these situations primarily out of fear. Alphas tend to find great comfort in their biological and marriage families and are very hesitant to "jump ship" for a male/male relationship that, in their minds, can only have an uncertain future. If the Alpha has children, the situation becomes even more complex and further reduces the chance that he will leave his family for another man—that is, unless he falls in love. It is often a love connection with another man that triggers the complex process of coming out for Alphas.

For Betas involved with a hidden or passing Alpha, I advise patience. If the connection between the two of you is real, there's a good likelihood that it will eventually work out. Additionally, many hidden Alphas feel content maintaining two relationships, and often their wives either directly or indirectly consent to these arrangements. Generally, in such arrangements, when push comes to shove, the wife and children will win out, so be prepared for holidays alone.

Of course, for those Betas who prefer to date men older than they are, there are usually plenty of Alphas in their thirties to choose from. If you are having trouble finding men your own age to date, perhaps looking in the decade above you will increase your number of potential partners.

For those Alpha males in their twenties who do come out, or are considering coming out, there is a very high chance that they will have their choice of partners, but must avoid the Alpha tendency to always seek more. Contrary to the Alpha's belief, a new guy isn't always sexier than the last one. Too often Alphas, finding such a large population of gay men to choose from, begin to cherry-pick, disqualifying men for any little issue. Forgiveness of another's flaws seems to be the first thing to go when there is an abundant supply of potential Beta partners for Alphas.

FOR MEN IN THEIR THIRTIES

As men enter their thirties, dating strategies begin to change. Betas begin to lose their greatest asset: their youth. Sadly, the prime mating age for Betas falls between eighteen and thirty-five. Alphas, just like their heterosexual brothers, prefer their partners to be in their reproductive prime, interestingly enough, considering that these pairings do not result in biological reproduction.

Betas

Dating strategies for Beta men in their thirties are dictated by this Alpha desire. As a result, we see many gay men in their thirties attempting to look younger, often wearing clothing that is, frankly, inappropriate for their age. Youth-oriented clothing lines such as Abercrombie & Fitch may be appropriate for young men, but by your mid-thirties, you run the risk of appearing to be "mutton dressed as lamb."

The best relationship advice I can give Betas in their thirties is to maintain your physical health *reasonably*, without becoming hypermasculine in appearance. Increasing your body size and mass by using steroids, aside from being dangerous, may actually backfire. Yes, you might get more sexual attention, but it will come from other Betas. And as odd as it may seem, Alphas desire men who are less manly than they are. Remember, a good model is Batman and Robin. Robin was not bigger than Batman, nor more powerful.

For the Beta male, your behaviors and actions should respond to the true, essential needs of a future partner. The most powerful draw for an Alpha is a man who displays a great joy in life, who is active, lively, even *vivacious*. If you surround yourself with other Betas, there is a good chance that the competition will be high among you for the few "good" men you encounter. By following the alternative plan of finding men in the real world, as outlined in an earlier chapter, you will greatly reduce the direct competition you'll find in a traditional gay situation. Beta men in their thirties who are seeking life partners would be well advised to seek men who are older than they are, as well as to keep their eyes open for missing Alphas who cross their paths.

Alphas

For Alpha men in their thirties, this is a good time to consider dating men who are also in their thirties, but slightly younger than you are, up to five years younger. While your sexual desires will naturally pull you toward men who are much younger than you, such as men in their teens and early twenties, most of these men are in no way ready to marry and settle down. Dating younger men is usually setting yourself up for heartbreak. Young Betas are still exploring their own personal power, and by the time they're in their early twenties, they will realize the incredible power that comes with their youth and beauty, as well as the limitations that an Alpha partner will put on them. Alphas are notorious for feeling threatened by the youth and beauty of their younger partners, but they may feel the most jealousy from the physical comparison their partner may make between the Alpha's body and the body of the Beta partner's new lover.

The greatest challenge for most Alphas in their thirties is overcoming their fears of "settling." There is a natural discomfort that comes to the surface for most Alpha males when confronted with the very real possibility of being married to one man for life. Alphas often pride themselves as being "lone wolves." This discomfort comes more from the idea of aging, and its limitations, than it does from what most people assume: the loss of outside sexual partners. Despite these behaviors, most Alpha men do prefer to be in a relationship as opposed to being alone. Once an Alpha has made a commitment to another, he tends to truly believe in it and holds fast to the relationship—unless he's tempted away by the sex appeal of a more youthful lover, which is always a threat. Persistent Betas, over time and with a strong hand, can successfully get an Alpha to make a commitment.

FOR MEN IN THEIR FORTIES

As men move into their forties, their bodies begin to show signs of aging. By far the most powerful aspect of aging for gay men (as it is for all men) is the lessening of testosterone. By natural design, testosterone beings to decline as we age in order to prepare us for less aggressive roles in our lives. As men age, they take on the softer role of grandfather, helping their own offspring take care of their offspring, thus giving further assurance that their genetic information will be passed on.

For most heterosexual men in their forties, this is a decade of success. The forty-plus man generally has met and married a woman, is succeeding in his career, and has produced a child or two. As his testosterone drops, the aggressive traits that were beneficial in his career make way for the more rational thought of upper management. His pursuit of women has decreased due to the natural decline of testosterone, other physical impacts of age, and the presence of children in the household. Thus, heterosexual men feel less need to continue the "search" for sexual partners.

The opposite is true for gay men, even those gay men in relationships. Contrary to straight men, gay men rarely have young children in their households, and the presence of another male in the household (as opposed to a wife) actually increases the competitive production of testosterone. The increase of competitive testosterone counterbalances the decline of testosterone due to aging. For Alphas in their forties, this higher level of testosterone can be a major source of conflict: a high desire to mate with a young man who turns up his nose at him because the Alpha in his forties is just too "old."

Alphas

What most forty-plus Alpha men fail to understand is that what they seek isn't a young, nubile body, but a young, nubile mind and personality—something that Betas of all ages possess. My dating advice for the Alpha in his forties is to widen his dating pool to include men he would not normally consider for life partners—in particular, men he considers slightly more feminine than he normally would date. Why? Because these men are no less men, and are much more likely to provide what he's actually seeking: men who are able to commit to him, respect him, and bring a new joy of life into his world, the trademarks of Beta men. In addition, Betas are less focused on the physical beauty of their partners, a benefit to the aging Alpha.

One warning, though: forty-plus Alphas should also be aware that, in general, Betas are more likely to have quick, non-emotional affairs. Younger Betas, with their higher levels of testosterone, are much more motivated to seek outside sexual gratification, even if they're deeply in love with their older Alpha mate. An older Beta, while still interested in outside sex, is less likely to actually follow through, mainly from the lack of motivating testosterone.

As Alpha men in their forties begin to show signs of aging, the decrease of testosterone affects not only their appearance but also their behaviors. To increase the level of testosterone and thus their attractiveness to Betas, the forties Alphas should work hard at maintaining their bodies through diet and exercise. Too many Alphas let themselves go at this age and, as a result, they increase their body fat, which in turns accelerates their loss of testosterone. Testosterone depletion is indicated by sluggishness, depression, and the presence of more body fat, especially in specific locations that increase the feminine appearance of the male body, such as on the waist, hips, upper shoulders, and neck.

Betas

As for Betas in their forties, they face a unique problem I'll call the Beta Dilemma. For the first time in their lives, they may be drawn to men younger than they are. Traditionally, Beta men are drawn to Alphas older than they are, primarily because these men are seen as more "adult." Yet, as Betas age, they find themselves attracted to younger Alphas. This trait can lead to confusing cross dating, an older Beta dating a younger Alpha. Though cross-pattern dating does occur in the heterosexual world (think of Demi Moore and Ashton Kutcher), it is rare,

I recently placed an ad on the Internet seeking a partner. After a few days I began reading some of the ads that were posted and came across one that sounded great—that was, until I saw that the guy who had written it was fifty-six. That turned me off.

I was really upset after I realized I was reading my own personal ad.

—*Howard, 56*

and rarely works. The same is true in the gay world. A Beta in his forties dating a much younger Alpha male rarely works and should be avoided to forgo potential heartbreak.

My dating advice for Betas in their forties is to avoid acting and dressing inappropriately for their age, and instead to highlight their positive Beta traits: loyalty, liveliness, support, and kindness. Generally, Betas in their forties should be looking for partners in their fifties and sixties.

FOR MEN IN THEIR FIFTIES

As we continue to age, our sexual needs may change but sex remains a key component in our lives, and our need for companionship rarely decreases. At this point in our lives, relationships continue to play an important role, with a partner being our key support, comfort, and companion.

With the continued lessening of testosterone as we age, the distinctions between Alpha and Beta men become less obvious, yet the two mating styles continue to play important roles in the formation and maintenance of healthy relationships.

Betas

Betas searching for a partner during this period of life continue to face the challenge of physicality versus personality. Alphas, not unlike heterosexual men, tend to be drawn to younger mates between eighteen and thirty-five, and to see themselves as mentors and protectors.

Most Betas at this stage of life have grown used to meeting their own needs and may hesitate saying they still need someone. Highlighting one's independence simply tells potential Alpha mates that they're not needed. To draw an Alpha to you, don't waste your time trying to compete physically with younger men. You'll lose. Instead, focus on highlighting your personality traits that Alphas enjoy: your sense of humor and your lively, positive attitude toward life. Above all, stress how much you get from your potential partner and how much you enjoy him, respect him, and need him.

Alphas

Alpha dating advice for the older man includes maintaining and highlighting your masculinity through clothing, attitudes, and physical activity. A key part of the attractive appearance for the Alpha is good posture. One of the hallmarks of an Alpha male is a strong, upright, and powerful appearance. Becoming bent over decreases your masculinity and appeal.

The Alpha male's mating drive has traditionally focused on physical expression through his sexuality. With a diminishing sex drive, though, companionship shifts into a higher position and should be a focus for your relationship. Intense sexual experiences on the level you had during your twenties are unlikely to occur, and younger partners tend to be an exercise in frustration.

Even so, many single Alphas in this age group find themselves drawn to young men. Young Betas may be attracted to these men, primarily as mentors, and may be willing to connect in some way, primarily sexually, in exchange for the stability, protection, and financial security the Alpha males bring to them. While some of these relationships may grow

The Red Skull: Fifty years ago, you were Dr. Vaselli's ridiculous idea. You remain a clownish symbol that no one cares about.

Captain America: I care.

The Red Skull: You care? Then come to me, my brother. Let us see if this heart of yours is stronger than my hate.

—*Captain America, 1990*

into something more profound and complete, in general they, too, often fall into resentment. Usually, the older Alpha male pays the price for these relationships, both financially and emotionally. The younger Beta is still in his prime mating age and will be ready and able to move back into the dating field without a problem.

The best potential partners for men fifty or older are lively, healthy Beta men in their forties and older. Instead of focusing on the physical qualities of potential mates, Alphas would be better served focusing on the personality traits that define Betas. The true rewarding relationship comes from being cared for, respected, and needed—all characteristics Beta men readily offer to their partners.

Regardless of age, once you have met your counterbalancing partner, the challenges to a successful relationship do not end. In the next part, we explore the needs and trials of day-to-day life in a superheroic relationship.

Part V

IN WHICH WE LEARN HOW TO MAINTAIN A SUCCESSFUL RELATIONSHIP

Our Hero looks out over the valley below him. All seems well, but he is unsure, feeling a need for vigilance.

CHAPTER 11

Creating a Superheroic Relationship That Lasts: Year 1 to Year 3

Voice: And so, it's easy to see why superheroes are at a cross-roads. Driven to succeed, yet encumbered by images of the traditional superhero icon, increasingly at odds with today's societal structure.

Space Ghost: Tell me about it.

Voice: Following are my seven superhero salvos for success. Repeat these at will.

Space Ghost: Alright.

Voice: Number one: I am in charge.

Space Ghost: I am in charge.

Voice: Number two: Mine is an energy that I choose to share.

Space Ghost: Mine is an energy that I choose to share.

Voice: Number three: Remember, no one can make you feel inferior without your consent.

Space Ghost: Oh, geez, what now?

—Space Ghost, "Coast to Coast"

I WANT YOU TO IMAGINE THIS: *any man* you've ever wanted (maybe someone you didn't even know you wanted) drawn to you, wanting you, needing you, matching your hopes and dreams almost as if by magic. He likes things about you even you don't care for. And he is so attractive, so kind, so smart, that you could *never* imagine someone like him being attracted to you. You're surprised, stunned, and amazingly happy. He doesn't mind if you call; he wants you to. He doesn't mind that you want to see him every second of the day; he feels the same way.

What the heck is going on here? You feel like a teenager, head over heels in—yes, that's what this is—love! You find yourself thinking about him and getting giddy. You imagine the next time you'll be together and you feel your pulse race. Love! At long last, love! The man you always fantasized about but was afraid was out of your league (or that he played on the other team, at least) is now lying next to you in bed. You read this book, you followed the guidelines, you made friends with him first, then you took a risk and acknowledged your desire for him, and last night, it happened: you connected! Finally, success! Or, at least, you think this is success.

Now, how not to screw this up!

SUCCESS! OR NOT…

How do you know when to trust your feelings? Too many times you've been fooled—convinced you had found Mr. Right, only to watch as he transformed right before your eyes into the Joker, the Riddler, or worse yet, Mr. Freeze, showing no emotion. Are there ways to ensure that it will work this time? Maybe. Perhaps a better way to approach this stage of mating is to see it for what it is: a trial run.

This isn't to deny the existence of love at first sight. I'm a true believer in it, and so are most couples who make it for a lifetime. (As I mentioned in the introduction, of those couples in our survey who lasted twenty years or longer, an amazing 100 percent reported that they fell in love at first sight.)

Yes, of course, these early feelings have to be backed up with many conscious decisions, but if you believe in love and the power of love at first sight, you'll be well on your way to success. Our long-term couples all described their first encounters as feeling very natural, as if the two were preordained to be together. Almost all these men reported the same experiences I just described: a racing pulse, giddy feelings, wanting to talk, to catch up, to discover each other anew. It all sounds so stereotypical because it is! This is the human experience of being in love, a feeling so powerful that it feels like a chemical high. And honestly, it is a chemical high, one brought on by a series of stimuli, all designed to ensure a strong bond, one that a full and complete marriage can be built on for the long term.

One of the primary problems I see in my couples work is people assuming that these early, powerful chemical feelings will last a lifetime, that they will forever feel as strongly as they did on Day 1. I'm sorry to say that you won't—but if you hang in there, something more profound and deep will evolve between you and your partner. Though there is something to be said for a shiny new piece of furniture, it can't compare to the beauty of an antique, a piece that carries a dark lustrous patina from years of use.

But that's in your future. Now your love is as bright as a shiny new penny. Enjoy it, yet at the same time, be aware of the three roadblocks that too often cause new relationships to end prematurely.

COMMON ROADBLOCKS TO SUCCESS

Fear of Femininity

I've mentioned the fear of appearing feminine before, and it often raises its ugly head early in relationships. At the beginning of the dating process, most men are on their best behavior, and for many men in our community this might mean limiting one's more gentle side. It isn't until we begin to establish a closer tie with someone that we feel safe enough to show our true colors.

Often, this fear of femininity comes wrapped in unusual issues. I have encountered this discomfort with femininity in obvious cases of traditional male/female roles in the household, such as who drives, who cooks, who does the laundry, and who takes out the trash. But more interesting have been cases where this fear has arisen in decision making. It's important never to assume who will make decisions in a new couple. All possibilities should be open to discussion, making sure that both partners are okay with the roles they have agreed to take on in the relationship.

How are decisions to be made? Jointly or independently? How does each man feel about the need to answer to the other? Will one feel resentment for the other's meddling into his affairs? It's easy to imagine the resulting situation: ongoing power conflicts and resentments. But what makes it more insidious is when there's an underlying concern about masculinity. If one partner is concerned about being seen as feminine, being asked to vacuum could be an invitation to a fight. It's important that couples discuss these feelings early in their relationship, and that both men feel assured that being more feminine or more masculine is not an issue in the relationship.

Unless it is. I have seen relationships collapse over the slightest sign of femininity in one of the partners. I had a client once who couldn't stand any hint of femininity in his partner. All was going great in their early weeks of wining and dining, until one night his newfound love asked if he could cook for him. That was too much for him, and he cut him off. Have we gotten to such a level of discomfort with all things nurturing that we can't see the incredible value a loving, gentle man brings to a family? It is important to understand that hypermasculine men tend to be unable to form lasting relationships, whereas men with a gentle edge are more far more willing to invest in a long-term commitment.

By far the most common complaint I hear from gay couples is not over household chores, though that does come up at times, but over this essential difference, the conflict between the feminine and the masculine. In our current gay community, we have been taught that being dependent, following someone else's lead, or being receptive rather than directing—all traits we see as feminine—are negatives in a relationship.

Gay men suffer a disproportionately high level of "femophobia": a fear of being feminine or being perceived as feminine. Gay men, when asked how feminine a man can be and still be considered for a relationship, said by a margin of 60 to 40 that they had to be "highly masculine." This is from men who described the average heterosexual man as simply "masculine." In other words, a large majority of respondents set a higher standard of masculinity for their potential mates than for the average straight guy, the gold standard for masculinity. The reason why may lie in the comment made by one of the respondents: "Though I see my partner as being very masculine, very manly, and sexy, my friends laugh when I say so." Perhaps masculinity is also in the eye of the beholder.

Our Broken Histories

The second challenge for gay men seeking to establish healthy relationships is that many of us carry a damaged psychological history. As we saw in the NMRS, gay men report high levels of mental illness, including depression, anxiety, and substance abuse. Understandable when you consider that we're one of the few minorities that isn't born into families of the same minority. Too often our histories as children form the basis for our adult relationships. If sexual and affectional feelings were uncomfortable or conflicted when we were children, often they remain troubling in adults.

If you want a healthy, long-term relationship, it's essential to free yourself from past guilt and confusion in order to create an adult connection now. If you have not already done so, now is a good time to consider a few psychotherapy sessions as a couple. Many men find themselves still carrying hurt feelings from being rejected as children, and approaching adult relationships in the same manner, as a hurt and rejected child. Other men bear the burden of the other side of these stories: harsh and rejecting bullies when male affection comes to them. Both positions are uncomfortable, and unnecessary. Counseling early in a relationship may seem unusual, even pointless, but periodic visits early on—say, every three or six months for the first two years—can establish a strong basis of communication and honesty that will serve the relationship well in the long run.

A Lack of Belief in Gay Marriage

The final issue I see among many gay men forming relationships is a belief in *gay relationships* but not in *gay marriage*. Too many gay men have an underlying suspicion about gay marriage, a belief that gay relationships are fun, flexible, and forgiving, and that they are somehow *less serious* than heterosexual marriage. Too often gay men enter into relationships as "trial runs" instead of as the lifelong marathons they truly are. The gay community's attitude about breakups certainly implies a less-than-serious outlook. You both must believe that there is a unique goodness to be found in a happy gay marriage and to take your commitment seriously.

From the study of evolutionary psychology, we know that nature does not create any process, social or physical, without some express purpose. The same can be said for gay relationships. There is a specific benefit for the individual (and for the species) in the establishment of such relationships. If we don't take our long-term relationships seriously, no one else will, either.

A great idea for every couple early in their relationship is to discuss what each one sees as his *vision of the purpose and function of the relationship,* with the goal of developing a shared vision. This vision should include common beliefs and values, as well as a basic understanding of what the purpose of the couple is to be. Is the relationship simply for sex? Is it to keep loneliness away? Is one of its purposes to be a political statement? What about the shared future? Do we plan to have children? What about careers? What about money?

Many couples dive in, assuming that all matters will be resolved on their own, and probably from their sole perspective. These early months are the perfect time to begin to build a shared vision of all the dreams you two will hold together, be it starting a business or building a family of dogs and kids.

One of the greatest benefits of being in a relationship is self-improvement, a process that is facilitated by the presence of a counterbalancing mate. Opposite traits provide a beneficial leveling effect to the couple. Say you have a temper that tends to run hot, especially one that has gotten you in trouble. You will naturally be drawn to a man whose nature is much calmer. In fact, this is one of the traits that you admire in him. Through your partnership with him, you will learn from his behaviors, as well as benefit from his calming nature in situations in which your temper gets the best of you. For your partner, perhaps his overly calm demeanor has allowed others to walk all over him. Your increased reaction is probably something he admires in you, as well as benefits from. You are each a better person from being associated with the other. Such is the nature of counter-balancing traits.

THE SUCCESSFUL COUPLE

Finally, here are eight early indicators of a gay couple on their way to a successful lifelong marriage:

- Those couples who make it tend to have met when they were younger, generally in what is known as the "mating years," between the ages of eighteen and thirty-five.
- These couples also have a strong Alpha/Beta balance between the two partners, with the Beta partner "melting" into the Alpha partner's life, more so than vice versa.
- Happy gay couples, just like heterosexual couples, tend to have strong common interests.
- These couples also have strong common universal values, with a high respect for gay marriage.
- The couples that make it in the long run tend to start off monogamous for the first two years or so, then realize that one or both partners desire sexual contact outside the relationship. After a period of limited outside sex, these couples tend to return to a happy, monogamous

Hadley: We read in Dear Abby once that we should never go to bed mad—that's bullshit. You want to know what the key to a long love life is? Three things: saying I love you, even when we don't feel it, forgiving each other's weaknesses, and always looking into each other's eyes when kissing. That'll keep you going, and sometimes, it'll actually get you going. [He grabs Matt's thigh]

Matt: And being married to a pervert doesn't hurt either...

—Matt, 75, and Hadley, 80 (together for 56 years)

relationship for the rest of their time together, though not with a formal agreement of monogamy.

- The partners in these couples believe in each other, and express an open pride in their partner's achievements.
- These couples trust each other, and express that trust by sharing all aspects of their lives, including money.
- And above all, these couples openly, and often, express their love and respect for each other, usually every day.

CHAPTER 12

Batman and Robin Forever: Year 3 and On

Batman (to Doctor Meridian): You trying to get under my cape, doctor?

Dr. Chase Meridian: A girl can't live by psychoses alone.

Batman: It's the car, right? Chicks love the car.

Dr. Chase Meridian: What is it about the wrong kind of man? In grade school it was guys with earrings. College, motorcycles, leather jackets. Now, oh, black rubber.

Batman: Try firemen, less to take off.

Dr. Chase Meridian: I don't mind the work. Pity I can't see behind the mask.

Batman: We all wear masks.

Dr. Chase Meridian: My life's an open book. You read?

Batman: I don't blend in at a family picnic.

Dr. Chase Meridian: Oh, we could give it a try. I'll bring the wine, you bring your scarred psyche.

Batman: Direct, aren't you?

Dr. Chase Meridian: You like strong women. I've done my homework. Or do I need skin-tight vinyl and a whip?

Batman: I haven't had that much luck with women...

—Batman Forever, 1995

FOREVER? Gay men are notorious for short memories, but those of us who want to be married once and for life will need to make a concerted effort through the years. All the years. Never assume that your relationship is "done." In this chapter, we highlight some special things you can do to assure the long-time success of your marriage. You may find some of these ideas old-fashioned, silly, or even pointless. So be it. I only report what I have seen in couples who have made it through the years, happily. Perhaps being open to the old-fashioned or the silly helps us make our way through the harsh realities of life.

COMMITMENTS

Can you honestly make a commitment to be with another person *forever?* For many of my clients, saying, with commitment, that they intend to be together forever is a challenge. I can understand that it may seem like a lot to ask anyone, but most research indicates that those men who do make these commitments are the men who end up staying happily together for thirty, forty, fifty years or more.

I can understand the hesitancy of some of my clients, though. I once read a book entitled *The Millionaire Next Door.* After reading it, and realizing what it took to be a millionaire, I decided that it really wasn't what I was looking for. Maybe you're feeling the same way about gay marriage. Maybe it's not your cup of tea. Yet, before you decide that's your final feeling on the subject, I would offer a different perspective. You're going to be surprised by how easy it is to be married. Yes, that's right: *it's easy to be married.*

When I was first dating guys, I remember how difficult it seemed to me to be with someone. I was trying so hard, working every angle, calculating each encounter with a new boyfriend, convinced that if things weren't perfect, I must have been doing something wrong. It wasn't until I got into a good

Alpha/Beta relationship that things really fell into place and, despite the inevitable problems that arose, it worked. With a few tweaks, it worked really well.

I'm always amused by people on TV talk shows who go on and on about the hard work one has to put into a marriage. Truth is, if you trust your natural instincts and let that system work for you instead of working against it, things will go pretty smoothly. It is those men who don't trust their guts, who constantly try to control all aspects of their lives and the lives of their partners, who end up facing divorce.

Of course, in every marriage there comes a time when one asks, "Is this really the person for me?" If you've managed to pass through the early stages of marriage, those years when everything is a new discovery, trust me: he's right for you. I rarely see couples who have made it past five years who aren't "right" for each other. For many of my clients, when the going gets tough in a relationship, instead of using the marriage for support, they turn *against* it and seek outside support. In that process, they destroy the marriage. A marriage that goes unused grows musty and pointless. Let me repeat that, because it is so important: when your marriage is in trouble, you should turn to your partner and ask for help with your problems instead of seeking an outside solution. Turning to a best friend or a new lover is never the solution. Talk to your life partner and, together, understand the issue and address it.

THE BETTER HALF OF ME: ADMIRATION, RESPECT, AND TRUST

The best advice I can give any couple, either heterosexual or gay, is to function within the three pillars of a healthy relationship: Admiration, Respect, and Trust. Yes, ART—loving another is truly an art form, one that can be taught and perfected.

Contrary to what clients are often taught by their therapists, I believe that brutal honesty has no place in a healthy marriage.

I don't know how people came to believe that it's okay to say *anything* that pops into your mind to the person closest to you. Healthy relationships are based first and foremost on respect. "I can tell you anything" is not the same as "I can say anything I want about you."

Many couples come to therapy under the assumption that the key to success is, as they put it, "honest communication." A key element of good communication is the ability to successfully and correctly get your message across. But people sometimes use the premise of honesty to say something that is hurtful and vindictive. Anything that needs to be said can be said in a kind and supportive way.

Partners who respect each other have a willingness to show consideration and appreciation for each other, deferring to the partner, sometimes even when they feel he's wrong. In a healthy relationship, it's completely appropriate to say you feel that your partner may be wrong, but it is *never* okay to say he's wrong and degrade him in the process.

During the early months of a relationship, you will find yourself flooded with admiration for your partner and he for you. This mutual admiration club need not end when the chemical rush of early love ends. One of the key success markers of happy couples is a feeling of admiration for their other half. Partners who make a daily effort to find something to admire about their spouses tend to stay together. Such admirations can go from the simple, "He's so cute when he's sleeping," to the sublime, "His actions make the world a better place." I am always struck by how happy couples always seem to find good things to say about each other. To acknowledge these good traits, especially out loud and in front of others, makes these observations even more powerful, tightening the bond between the two of you. But for many gay men, paying compliments is difficult, primarily because of testosterone competition (discussed later).

Finally, trust is fundamental to a successful lifelong relationship. Trust is a tricky thing in many gay relationships, mainly because it requires one to go against a basic male trait: control. If you say you trust someone, you are in essence saying, "I allow you to be in control." If you say to a driver, "I trust you behind the wheel of the car," you are saying you believe he will not harm you; in essence, you are giving him control over your life.

In a marriage, you place your trust in your partner; you give up control of hundreds, if not thousands, of aspects of your life. This type of trust is as simple as "I trust you'll be home for dinner" to as complex as "I trust you to take care of me if I become incapacitated." In order to trust your partner, you must believe in him. You must think that he is your equal in his ability to manage both his life and yours. Your relationship is a partnership in which both parties have the welfare of the marriage in mind. Both partners should be acting in a manner that is supportive of the relationship's success, as opposed to his individual success. In order for this to happen, both partners must be willing, and able, to give up control to some degree. Often this means giving up control over issues that you might find particularly hard to let go of: sex, money, and power.

In order to have a successful relationship, gay men must learn to share. All healthy relationships are a triad: you, your partner, and the relationship itself. To find success in the long run, couples must actively create the third entity—the "our" part: our money, our sex life, our future, our home, our thoughts, our feelings. Without the establishment of a "we" in a relationship, most relationships will fail.

RELATIONSHIP STAGES

Within the heterosexual community, there is a pretty clear process, a series of stages that a man and a woman pass through as they move from single to married. In the gay community, there have been few such signposts to measure the progress of the relationships. As a result, many gay men have difficulty understanding where they are in the process. Outlined below is the path that gay relationships generally follow over a lifetime.

First Date

Just as with straight men and women, gay men begin the process of finding a life mate by dating. But while heterosexuals on average wait until the fifth date for first sexual contact, gay men tend to engage in sex their first or second time together.

First Month

Heterosexual couples, once they have had sex, also move into a stronger relationship, announcing their relationship to friends as boyfriend and girlfriend. Gay men tend to fall into two different camps at this point. Some are still hesitant to announce to friends that they are "boyfriends" and continue to take the less committed position, saying, "I had a date with…" or "I'm seeing someone." At the other extreme are men who immediately move into the position of being a lifelong couple, often claiming this is "the one." Both positions can be dangerous. I would recommend that couples at this stage use the "boyfriends" tag to identify their relationship as moving forward, but not too quickly.

First Month to First Year
(Dating Exclusively)

At this stage, heterosexual couples tend to move into an exclusive dating agreement, seeing only each other. For many gay men, this is a period of discomfort and questioning. Often afraid of being limited by the relationship, some gay men fight the need for commitment. It is essential, however, that during this time the couple foster a safe, noncompetitive monogamy, at least until the relationship is strongly established. One key function of this period of the relationship is the continuing growth of expectation for a future together. Many gay couples find themselves stuck in this stage, their relationship neither moving forward to full commitment nor ending. Such "limbo" relationships will be frustrating to one or both partners.

Six Months to One Year (Commitment)

During these months, the couple moves from exclusive dating to a point where the relationship grows to the first major shared decision: "What is our intention? Are we serious about being a couple?" If the answer is yes, the gay couple tends to move in together. If the answer is no, the relationship tends to end at this point. The next few months together are a time of engaging in the first joint responsibilities, such as establishing a joint checking account, looking for an apartment together, and other shared decision making, decisions that are generally comparable to a heterosexual couple's decision to try living together or to become engaged to marry.

For many gay couples, this ends the obvious transition from single to married, unlike heterosexual couples, who pass through additional stages designed to provide socially approved means of ending or continuing the relationship (engagement and wedding). The danger for gay couples is the lack of additional time to "try out" each other, as well as socially acceptable ways to end a relationship.

RECOMMENDED FUTURE STAGES FOR THE GAY COUPLE

Engagement (Six Months to One Year)

I recommend that gay couples follow a path to marriage that is similar to the path followed by heterosexual couples. Doing so allows the couple access to socially accepted ways either to end a relationship that is not working or to build support for formal recognition of, and support for, the permanence of the relationship. Following such a path of recognition builds an expectation in the couple, and in the couple's support system, that once the relationship passes a given point, it is expected to last a lifetime. Instead, though, many gay men at this stage move into a type of "temporary marriage," living together with an understanding that they are "trying" to make it forever, yet with no real commitment.

Private Commitment (at the End of the Engagement)

Once the trial engagement period has ended, couples must ask each other if they are willing to make a lifelong commitment. If the answer is yes, the couple moves on to the next step, a public commitment. If either party answers no, the relationship ends. If either partner is unsure but wants to continue the relationship, it moves into a state of limbo, unsure of its purpose.

Public Commitment (Usually Within a Year of Private Commitment)

At this stage, couples must begin to identify themselves within their social circle and family as a couple for life, often by calling themselves "married" or "partners." An essential and powerful tool for publicly identifying as a couple for life is a public commitment ceremony. Such ceremonies not only provide a milestone for life but also increase the likelihood of success for a long-term relationship. At this point, the couple declares themselves a married couple and expects to be treated as such.

Establishment of the Public Couple (Ongoing)

The ultimate stage of a healthy marriage is the establishment of the public couple through an ongoing series of processes through which the couple, for example, combines financial resources, jointly purchases property, creates legal documents that declare end-of-life decisions, legally changes names to reflect the relationship, and in other public ways claims the legitimacy of the relationship.

The Importance of Public Ceremonies

One of the best ways to help reduce the possibility of a breakup during the two- to five-year danger zone may seem obvious, but is often overlooked: a wedding. Almost all major life transitions are marked with ceremony. Weddings, bar mitzvahs, graduation processions, birthday parties, and funerals all are designed to allow for public recognition of a moment of particular significance. From single to married, from life to death, from child to adult, at all points of transition, we have ceremonies designed to allow people to move from one set of rules and expectations to another.

Generally, as we partake in these ceremonies, there is some form of agreement through which participants are asked to take on new responsibilities. Those of us who participate as witnesses agree to assist those making the transition in meeting these new obligations. But for many gay men, the transition from single to married goes by with merely a mention to friends. "I'm seeing a new guy" does not make a strong foundation for a major life transition. Such hidden transitions do not fulfill their intended roles. There is no opportunity for a public statement of commitment and acceptance of the responsibilities that come with such a statement, nor is there any request for public support. No wonder it's so easy to break up.

Often, gay men use moving in together as a marker of transition, but this can have all the feelings of a real estate transaction: "We'll see if it works out…" With a public ceremony, there's not only a commitment to making a marriage work but also the added support of those around you who witnessed the

When I was in high school, in 1972, we were shown a movie called *Future Shock*. One of the scenes it showed was a gay wedding. Two guys in crushed baby blue velvet, as I recall. Anyway, the narrator said something about gay marriage occurring by the turn of the twenty-first century. My class reacted with revulsion, cat calls, all that. I remember the discussion being one of total disbelief—there was no way gay marriage would ever occur, and certainly not within twenty-five years or so.

Well, on January 1, 2000, my partner and I stood before our priest and declared our eternal love for each other. I couldn't help but think about the historic reality of all of this. Though our marriage isn't legally recognized yet, it was profound for us, as well as for those who attended. We were all crying, in happiness, but also in recognition that we were doing something beyond ourselves.

—Dax, 52

declaration of commitment. Significantly, along with that public support comes public pressure to take the responsibilities and commitments of marriage seriously. Though many may scoff at such public statements, and though they certainly have not guaranteed the success of heterosexual marriages, their effect on those of us who have stood before a crowd and declared our intentions is very powerful. If we expect people to treat our relationships with the same respect they give heterosexual marriages, we must agree to take them seriously ourselves, not just "through health, for richer, and for only as long as the fun lasts." Every couple should be able to identify some point, some place, as the moment they went from being single to married. And meant it.

THE COUPLE DESTINED FOR SUCCESS

We can now draw a profile of the gay couple most likely to see old age together. This is what that couple looks like:

Two men, one with an Alpha mating style, the other with a Beta mating style, and whose essential difference scores counterbalance each other. They understand that this difference brings balance, a yin and a yang, to their relationship, with each partner having their strengths and weaknesses. Neither partner considers one weaker than the other. They both value and respect these differences and understand that, at times, one partner will have to agree, perhaps against his honest beliefs, to accept his partner's position. They agree to trust the judgment of the other. They trust their partner to manage their lives, including sharing their finances and making decisions about life and death when they're unable to do so themselves. These men share common universal beliefs about money, child rearing, and religion, and come from closely related socio-economic classes and cultural backgrounds. They also share a fair number of daily interests. They have made a conscious decision to be together for the rest of their lives and accept the limits that such an agreement puts on them as individuals, understanding that the benefits outweigh the limits. They are comfortable accepting the ambiguities that come with the constantly changing situation that is marriage. They have intentionally presented themselves as, and have made a public statement that they are, a couple for life. They have asked for support for this relationship from their families, friends, and peers. And above all, they believe in the power of their long-term love to overcome any temporary problems that might come their way.

Is this you? If so, I have full confidence in your future together. That's not to say you won't face problems. All couples do, and for gay men these problems can be pretty predictable, often being based on misunderstandings of the Alpha/Beta differences. In the next chapter, let's take a look at the most common problems gay couples will face in their lives together.

CHAPTER 13

"Batman Driven Crazy with Jealousy— Destroys Gotham!": Dealing with Problems

TROUBLE IN PARADISE? Contrary to popular belief, problems in a marriage are rarely signs that the marriage is doomed to fail, even if we never saw Batman and Robin fighting with each other. Marriages tend to fail when problems are either ignored or given too much power, thus problems in a marriage are simply a sign of engagement. Marriages without some form of disagreement tend to be weak, surface relationships. In this chapter we look at the most common forms of conflict that come up in gay relationships, and suggest some simple ways to reconsider these differences.

Problems that occur between partners in gay relationships almost always have a basis in the Alpha/Beta dynamic. As would be expected, men with an Alpha disposition approach life, and its challenges, from a different angle than Beta men do. In general, as we have seen, Alphas have a strong problem-solving attitude, while Betas are more open with the emotional, personal side of life. A common problem that I often see is a dispute over who makes decisions—not the major decisions that come up, but the simplest day-to-day decisions.

For example, I saw a couple in my practice because they could not agree on who was to do the laundry. Though it might seem a simple issue, this couple was really trying to resolve larger questions of responsibility, equality, and decision making. The Alpha partner, when he did assist with the laundry duties, felt (and acted) as if he were doing his partner a favor, whereas the Beta partner felt doing the laundry was a shared necessity, not a favor to him. Of course, the Beta partner's attitude came across as "bitchiness" and ungratefulness for any help he received. And this camouflaged bigger problems. Was it the Beta partner's responsibility to maintain the household? Was he being treated as the housewife? If so, was he comfortable with that role and its responsibilities? The Alpha partner, who was the primary breadwinner in the household, felt that he did his part by bringing in more money. Once we discussed the inner conflicts in their relationship and began to rebalance the power within the relationship, the issue of the laundry began to fade.

Let's move to a discussion of the most common problems that arise between gay couples, from the perspective of the Alpha/Beta dynamic, and some potential resolutions.

MATCHING TYPE

Many of the problems I see in my practice come down to one simple problem: matched mating styles. Couples in which both men are Betas tend to come into therapy when they can't take the boredom anymore. Beta/Beta couples are like best friends—sisters, almost. They enjoy each other's company, find they have lots in common, and have boring sex. Both men in Beta/Beta relationships tend to find themselves desiring and probably acting on outside sexual interests. The primary danger here is that since the boredom has grown high between the two partners, when seeking outside sex, these Beta men may seek hypermasculine sex partners, often in unsafe situations. Many times these men will become involved with heterosexual men, the ultimate Alphas in their minds, and find themselves disappointed when the relationship goes nowhere, or harmed if it ends violently.

Alpha/Alpha couples face a different set of problems. Since Alpha men take relationships seriously, they may find themselves torn by their conflicted feelings, wanting to stay married yet finding that the level of conflict continues to grow. Two Alpha men in a household tends to lead to constant bickering, fights breaking out over almost any little thing. The strongest component in an Alpha/Alpha relationship is sex. Once the initial stage of sexual engagement ends, usually within the first two years, these relationships begin to show their wear. Combine a waning sex life with increasing arguments and these relationships collapse fairly quickly. Both men find themselves seeking sex outside the relationship.

Solutions to the same-match problems? Know your mating style and the mating style of your future partner before you get in over your head. Though it may seem like a "perfect match" in the early stages, eventually these similarities will make their way to the surface and begin to damage the relationship.

LIVING TOGETHER

According to the U.S. Census, 95 percent of married heterosexual couples live together. Not true for gay couples. In both our 2006 survey and a 1996 survey of gay couples conducted by the National Gay and Lesbian Task Force, only about 65 percent of gay couples live in the same house. Why is this important? Of those couples who'd been together for more than twenty years, 100 percent reported sharing a home from early in their relationship. Those couples who had never lived with a spouse or partner were much more likely to have broken up within five years.

This could be reflective of two things. First, couples who are attempting long-distance relationships can't live together,

If I could tell young gay couples anything, it would be this: Don't worry so much about those feelings that come at times, those feelings that you hate your partner. [He laughs.] Trust me, there are plenty of days, sometimes weeks, when you hate each other. If we had broken up every time we had strong emotions, we'd never have made it past the first year. But here we are looking at forty years together.

—*Bernie, 75*

and therefore miss out on the benefits of daily contact. The second possibility is that such couples failed to establish a "we," a shared intention, a sense of being one. Either way, they're forgoing the benefits of a shared household.

FADING FEELINGS

Many gay couples feel that once the intensity of the early years begins to fade, they are "falling out of love." In fact, it's a sign that their relationship is maturing, that the chemical (PEA) that is present during the initial "honeymoon" period of a relationship is slowly being replaced by the bonding hormones (oxytocinthe and vasopressin). Managing this transitional period proves difficult for many men, and the best advice for couples is to understand what is occurring and to know that it doesn't necessarily indicate a failing relationship, then to realize that the best way to approach this problem is with simple resolve.

Every relationship passes through times when both partners will question it. You must be open and willing to hear your partner talk about his concerns and to set your own fears aside to acknowledge his. The best response to a partner who says, "I'm not sure this is the right relationship for me" is to say, "I feel that way sometimes, but after thinking about it, I know I want to be with you. But I can certainly understand your concerns. It doesn't feel very good to wonder, does it?" I know it all sounds like a lot of "therapist-speak," but if you don't stay open to talking about the problem, these fears take on a life of their own. And an unspoken fear begs to be acted upon. Remember the question isn't only "Is this the right relationship for me?" but also "Is there someone else who would make me happier?" You don't want your partner moving from the first question to the next before the two of you talk.

SHARING MONEY

The stickiest topic for every couple is probably money. Gay couples are no different, but with a twist. Whereas heterosexual couples fight over how their money is spent or saved, gay couples fight over who brings in what. For a gay couple moving from dating into marriage, it's impossible to ignore the realities of money. To run a household, to run a life, we must have and manage money. The question for gay men, of course, is whose money?

Here is the most radical advice I will give you: pool your money. Just as a shared home is essential to establishing a "we," an understanding of "our money" is also important. Few gay couples bring in equal amounts of money. The contortions gay couples go through to remain "fair" in money transactions would be humorous if they weren't so damaging to these relationships. Money is nothing more than an indicator of power. And as with so many things in this book, the issue of money is colored by the Alpha/Beta dynamic.

In many happy relationships, there is an obvious disparity between the income the Beta partner provides and the amount the Alpha partner brings in. This is less of a problem in cases where the Beta partner is a lower earner than his Alpha partner, but in couples where the Beta partner brings in more income, conflicts can erupt. Another major problem can result from the Alpha/Beta difference, and is much more common. This problem usually arises when an Alpha partner has a higher income and expects his Beta partner to either match his contribution or to bring in a "percentage balance." That means that one partner may bring in 20 percent of the household income and his partner may bring in 80 percent; the Beta partner is allowed control over his 20 percent, while the Alpha maintains control over his 80 percent. The obvious problem with such an arrangement, while it may make sense on the surface, is a degrading power play between the two partners. Having control over 80 percent of the couple's income means that the Alpha is also exerting 80 percent of the couple's decision-making power. "Shall we buy a house?" in such situations becomes, in actuality, "Shall I buy a house and let you help me pay for it?"

Any relationship in which money is not controlled equally, regardless of how much each contributes, is damaged by these arrangements. Anything other than pooled money results in "my money versus your money," and the all-important "our" is lost.

THE TESTOSTERONE EFFECT: QUIEN ES MAS MACHO?

There was a skit on *Saturday Night Live* years ago entitled "Quien es mas macho?" that was supposed to be a Mexican game show that asked the contestants to choose which man pictured was more macho. It was a pretty funny skit. It was also an example of a damaging dynamic often seen in gay relationships, as each guy tries his best to be the more masculine, the more sexual, the more macho partner in the couple.

One of the biggest challenges to a male/male relationship is testosterone. Times two. Testosterone naturally triggers a man's desire to mate, to search for mates, and to compete for mates.

The gay household increases testosterone production and thus increases the need to seek and compete for other men. So not only is your partner a partner; he's also a competitor for other men you may encounter.

Testosterone, the hormone that increases a man's sexual drive, as well as his competitive nature, is triggered by the presence of other men, especially in situations of competition for sex partners. In heterosexual men, there is a natural rise in blood testosterone levels when meeting a new potential sex partner. If you add other men to the situation, the increase in testosterone in all the men is even greater.

The implications are obvious. Two men living in close proximity, with continued contact with other gay men, all of whom could be considered potential sexual conquests, is a formula for disaster in a relationship.

The length of time most gay men stay together indicates how easily we fall into the pattern of chemically induced short-term relationships, lasting around four or five years. The challenge for those gay men who desire a longer, even a lifelong, relationship is to understand these chemical phenomena and learn how to manage them.

When you place yourselves in an environment in which men compete for the attention of other men, such as a nightclub, bar, or bathhouse, you both will be naturally excited due to the higher level of testosterone stimulus. I have had clients report to me that they have met men at bathhouses and had "incredible sex," only to find the same person disappointing once they started seeing each other in everyday life. The same can be said about the highly sexual atmosphere of many men-only bars. Obviously, if one hopes to preserve a male/male relationship, the partners need to agree to limit the amount of time they spend in highly male-stimulating environments.

So here are some tips:

- Do not go to the baths together.
- Do not hang out at gay bars together.
- Limit your friendships with other gay males.
- Remember that every gay male you encounter is a potential sexual and emotional competitor for your partner's affections, even those in relationships themselves.
- Foster friendships with heterosexual married couples. I have found in the lives of my clients that those male couples who report having a heterosexual couple as best friends tend to be much more likely to survive past the first five years.

In situations where men normally gather in groups, such as in male-only dorms or in the military, testosterone levels lead to a highly charged environment, often with sexual overtones. The gay community is no different. If you are to visit almost any gay bar, peruse any gay male magazine or newspaper, or visit a gay dinner party, there will be an air of sexuality. For the male couple, this heightened level of stimulation can be dangerous to their relationship.

Competition for potential mates often results in the cattiness, confrontation, and backbiting that are all too common in the gay community. But what happens when you throw a happy gay couple into that environment? The same thing. As each partner checks out the scene and sees attractive and available men, testosterone levels in each naturally rise. While straight men may experience a similar phenomenon when they enter a singles bar, they do not face the unique situation that gay men face—competing against their own feelings of love, as well as their own partner, for the attention and approval of other potential sexual and emotional partners.

In married heterosexual partners, the man's testosterone is regulated by the presence of a female in the house. A woman does not stimulate competition the way another man does. Male testosterone levels drop even more in households with children. For gay couples without a female regulator or children, testosterone levels remain high. While this may be good for sexual activity between partners in a relationship, in the presence of other potential partners, both sexual and emotional, the competitive nature of heightened testosterone levels triggers intense and often combative emotions.

To make matters worse, these emotions are often in conflict. A man who sees his partner check out someone else may feel immediately competitive, angry, and combative, but also rejected, hurt, and unattractive. These conflicting emotions can lead to a rather aggressive reaction by one or both partners. One can easily see how both would be motivated to have sex with an outside partner—primarily to prove to themselves, as well as to their partner, that they still have the power to draw a potential partner.

In turn, such an action also allows you to punish your partner, making him feel the hurt and rejection that he made you feel. It also allows you to tell your partner, in an indirect way, that he had better stay in line, or you and your resources will be gone from his life. But in a gay relationship, there's a catch-22: he can do the same to you.

In order for a couple to survive, testosterone competition must be regulated. But how? Every couple must make a decision about how to handle sexuality in their relationship. Beyond the simple question of monogamy or open relationship, sexuality and the emotional competition it can bring can be very dangerous to the long-term survival of a relationship.

The first step for most couples is early in the relationship, when monogamy must rule. Most relationships are fragile in their first year or two, and during this time, it is best for couples to limit the possibility of outside sex. Most of my clients have found it beneficial to place limits on outside sexual expression during the first two years of a relationship. Many couples agree not to have sex with anyone else for the first two years, yet leave an opening for outside sex in the future. This provides two benefits: security during the fragile beginning of a partnership and freedom from the fear of being locked into a sexually unfulfilling relationship forever.

Limiting sexuality in the beginning of a relationship should also mean limiting expressions of sexual arousal by others, including cruising others in front of each other, saying someone is "hot," or maintaining any relationships or friendships that exclude your partner.

Another way to limit testosterone competition in your relationship is to limit the amount of time you and your partner spend in sexually stimulating environments. A couple that ventures into a bathhouse together is basically saying that they will engage in sex, either together or apart. As soon as they begin to walk the hallways, the competition begins, with each partner sizing up other potential partners, just as other men are sizing them up, individually and as a couple. The potential for problems is manifest: from rejection to an intense emotional connection, especially when either of these happens to one of the partners but not the other. I have had clients tell me that such adventures have gone well until one says to the other, "This guy thinks I'm hot, but isn't into you."

A bathhouse is an obvious example, but whenever gay men gather together without a strong presence of women and heterosexual men, there is a heavy scent of sexuality in the air. And it makes sense, of course: sexually available men stimulate the production of testosterone, and testosterone stimulates sexual thoughts and behaviors.

As I mentioned, gay couples can increase their chance of survival by having a straight couple for best friends. Another way is by reducing the amount of sexual stimulation in their lives, including the stimulation provided by pornography. There is a belief in the general community that exposure to pornography stimulates abuse against women, that men who look at stimulating images are more likely to act out their desires, by force if necessary. While there is a slight bit of evidence to support this idea, the truth is a bit more specific. Men who are stimulated and then presented with an opportunity to act do act more often than men who are stimulated but have no outlet for those desires.

In other words, if a gay man watches a movie of a man making a delivery to a house, and in the movie the delivery man then has sex with the resident, the next time this guy is at home when a delivery man rings his bell, he will be more likely to try to initiate sex than a man who had not seen the film. Why? What we see in movies tends to translate from "fantasy" into "possible." But there's the rub. In situations where fantasies can easily become reality, we are always more willing to act.

The lesson for gay couples is to limit erotic situations. Watching an erotic DVD together may increase the likelihood of sex between the two of you. Watching an erotic DVD with another gay couple increases the likelihood of the four of you having sex. The same can be said for a variety of sexual situations in the gay world. Couples have to agree on setting limits on sexuality, and agree to follow them.

Couples who limit or reduce their exposure to potentially sexual situations reduce the likelihood of sexual and emotional competition coming into play in their partnership. Partners should agree to limit visits to all-male environments, including gay bars and bathhouses, to foster friendships with heterosexual couples and families with children, and to limit their exposure to sexual stimulants, such as personal ads or online chat rooms. Doing so reduces the possibility that one or both of the partners will violate their agreement.

COMPETITION

As would be expected in any situation in which two men are involved, the issue of competition comes to the forefront for many gay couples. Yet often these fighting couples don't realize that their competitive nature is at play. Such is the ironic nature of being gay. We see ourselves as noncompetitive, and many of us have a history of avoiding traditional male-dominated sports because we were not very good at them.

But even in non-sporting events, competition comes into play. For gay men, and for all men, the greatest competition is for potential mates. This competition, though most obvious in sexual situations, can cause problems in a variety of ways, from something as innocuous as the way one dresses to being concerned about how attractive your partner is and how that reflects on you. In general, Beta men are much more susceptible to highly competitive urges, with the competition between the Beta partner and other Betas in the community leading to many dramatic conflicts.

As we discussed, the dynamic of mate competition between two gay men is sexual, intense, and complex, mainly as the result of increased levels of testosterone. The process is a string of stimulations, leading to higher levels of testosterone, which in turn stimulate even higher levels of testosterone.

Such a situation would appear like this: A couple enters a situation in which many attractive gay men have gathered, such as a gay bar. Immediately, the mating hunt begins, even if the couple has no intentions of connecting. As the couple walks into the bar, the other patrons scan them. Each partner is aware that he is being checked out, which triggers a reflexive hormonal response. It's exciting to be considered. Such stimulation encourages the partners to return the gazes, sending a subtle eye signal to certain men whom they, too, find attractive. Each partner will be aware that the other partner is stimulated by this situation, and will have a dual response: sexual arousal and competitive repulsion. This dual response, both of which trigger an increase in androgens, is because two outcomes are possible: their partner could choose to have sex with one of their new suitors and include them (sexually arousing), or they could try to get the suitor for themselves (thus competing against their own partner for the new suitor's attention and approval).

This process is confusing at best. Many couples become overwhelmed and angry. Alphas in these situations become possessive, often claiming that their Beta partners are flirting. Betas, for their part, tend to resort to negative baiting of the competition: running down any potential suitors who they feel threaten their position with their partners. Alpha men are much more likely to become physically aggressive in these situations, whereas Beta men will resort to more passive means, such as crying or degrading others. But even Betas, at times, given enough testosterone stimulation, will resort to physical aggression. As many men report, sex after fighting is great—it should be, since you're flooded with testosterone at the time.

Such sexual situations are the most obvious examples of this inner partner competition. More subtle forms can be seen when issues of appearance come up. I remember one couple fighting over what the other was going to wear when they went out. "You're not going to wear that, are you?" may not sound like the beginning of a competition, but it is based in the competitive urge. As is the case with almost every problem seen in gay couples, a single issue is commonly doubled by the presence of two men.

Here's what I mean. The question of appearance is twofold. The first question is, Will others find me attractive? The second question is, Will others find my partner attractive, thus confirming my power to draw the best partner to me? Donald Trump doesn't need his appearance to draw a trophy wife to his side (obviously!). But for him, a young, beautiful wife is a sign of his power to attract the best mate. A gay man needs to be young, handsome, and sexy to draw the best mate, and his mate must reflect his attractiveness by being just as young, handsome, and sexy. It's a delicate balancing act, because any sign of inequality between the partners, such as one being cuter than the other, results in a competition between the partners. This competition then triggers the type of conflict we saw above.

The need to manage attractiveness bleeds over into almost all aspects of gay life. For Beta men, whose primary tools for attracting mates are their bodies and their youth, concerns about appearances center upon the physical: clothing, facial and skin care, and trends of the young. This explains the fascination with youth culture, such as the images presented in Abercrombie & Fitch ads, for many gay men. Maintaining a connection to this part of life also maintains a lifeline to security and love for these men.

For Alpha men, interests are primarily in possessions, such as cars, real estate, and other tangible signs of success in business. Like their heterosexual male counterparts, Alpha men know that their success in love and in life depends on being able to provide for the security and well-being of their youthful, and at times fickle, partners.

This dance of appearances plays out in both the heterosexual world and the homosexual world. Women, like Betas, strive to maintain their youth in order to maintain their power over men. Heterosexual men strive to increase, and display, their resources so they can maintain power over young, beautiful women. Alphas strive to maintain their resources in order to retain their power to draw attractive, sexy young men.

The way this competitiveness plays out is different for Alpha men and Beta men. An Alpha will tend to desire a partner who is his equal financially, or is willing to balance out his income in a proportionate manner. For Betas, who often pursue low-paying careers in caregiving, teaching, or the arts, this can be problematic. I often hear Alphas avoiding good potential mates because they are afraid of being used for their incomes. One client said to me that all the men he fell for ended up being "gold diggers looking for a sugar daddy," when in fact many of these men simply did not make the money he thought they should.

For Betas, the problem plays out in a manner consistent with their natures: physically. Betas complain about their partners' failure to maintain appearances, such as not dressing well or not maintaining their lifestyle. Often as their Alpha partners begin to age and lose their physically attractive masculine appearance due to decreasing testosterone levels, Betas lose interest in them.

What is the solution to the competition problem? First, those partners who want to stay together, as was suggested before, need to avoid situations that could trigger a competitive episode. This is especially true for couples who are highly competitive sexually. For other situations where competition becomes an issue, such as with appearances, the first step to controlling these urges is to understand them, to know they are biologically based, and to realize that you can manage them, but not get rid of them.

JEALOUSY

An offspring of competition is jealousy. Evolutionarily, jealousy was intended to assist in maintaining familial units. For a heterosexual man, jealousy was a way to keep his female spouse attached to him, so she didn't reproduce with another male while expending his resources. Women, on the other hand, used jealousy to keep their primary mate in line, making sure to keep a provider and protector around to assure the well-being of their offspring. Today, a similar pattern can be seen among gay men.

Alphas tend to feel jealousy less than Betas do, usually only when their partner takes an interest in other Alpha men—especially if the other Alpha male is a threat to his status as provider and protector. A common example of ways Alphas try to lure away other Alphas' mates is to offer signs of their wealth and the security that such wealth could bring the Beta. Jealous Alpha men tend to use aggression, including an aggressive rejection of the Beta partner, to control situations in which they feel jealousy. If an Alpha finds that his partner has broken their agreement of monogamy, or just accepted gifts, a common reaction is to throw the Beta partner out of their home. The Alpha partner usually can exert that power because he controls the financial well-being of the household, and thus feels empowered to exert control as he sees fit.

Betas tend to feel jealous when another man threatens their security. This is commonly seen when other Beta males are sexually attracted to their partners. Betas tend to respond to such situations with some anger toward their partner, but knowing that threatening their partner could result in their being thrown out, most Betas will respond with obvious anger and passive aggression toward the other Beta suitor, hiding or replacing their anger toward their Alpha partner. A common response to such jealous feelings is for the Beta mate to disparage the character or appearance of the new suitor. Betas are notorious for their "bitchiness," and jealousy can bring this negative Beta trait to the forefront.

The situations that trigger jealousy in Alphas tend to differ from those that trigger jealousy in Betas. Alphas find their partner's sexual encounters outside their relationship much more threatening than an outside emotional connection. Betas, on the other hand, are more concerned by their partner's emotional attachments to others. If we consider the evolutionary history behind the emotion of jealousy, such attitudes make sense. Alphas are wired to keep a physical mate, while

Betas are wired to maintain a providing mate. Any emotional ties outside the relationship supplant the emotional connection that the Beta finds essential: the secret connection that only true lovers have. Often, Betas also see their partner's jealousy as an indication of their partner's feelings for them. This can be a dangerous game, as too much jealousy can lead to controlling behaviors, and even violence. Alphas, on the other hand, will stress the "sacred" connection that is broken when their partners have sex outside their relationships.

As a result of these different reactions, Betas are more likely to forgive their partners for straying, but are unlikely to forget, afraid that their partners could leave at any time. Alphas, on the other hand, are much more likely to view any transgression by their partners as a sign of moral weakness. If they do agree to remain in a relationship after a Beta transgression, the Alpha partner normally forgets about the transgression.

Straight men and Alpha gay men use aggression to keep potential suitors away from their mates. Straight women and Beta gay men use passive-aggressive traits, such as demeaning gossip, to control suitors. In societies where women outnumber men, such passive-aggressive behaviors increase, with women using them against other women. In societies where men outnumber women, violence increases, with men using violence against other men.

According to our survey, the majority of gay men believe that the worst thing about other gay men is their "cattiness, bitchiness, and gossiping," all of which are behaviors particularly associated with Betas. As our survey numbers have shown, the ratio of Beta men to Alpha men in the out community is high, almost 3 to 1. This limited availability of Alpha men, the best potential mates for the large Beta population, can perhaps explain the high level of negative Beta behaviors among gay men.

Can you imagine a gay community completely different from ours today? One where Alphas would outnumber Betas by almost 3 to 1? Instead of the stereotypical image of a bunch of aging old men sitting around a piano dishing each other, while each is secretly hoping a hot, masculine, "hard-to-believe-he's-gay" guy would walk through the door, we'd have a bunch of macho Alphas, drunk and depressed at seeing the same old Alpha guys every weekend, starting a fight over some hot, sexy Beta walking through the door. It would be our world, turned upside down. Instead of cattiness, though, we'd see an increase in fistfights at gay bars.

Solutions to jealousy require some thought, literally. When feeling jealous, start by realizing that this is a natural reaction, not an irrational thought process but a true, organic response to a perceived danger. For Alphas, that danger is potentially losing a mate to another, more powerful and sexual partner. Betas will feel jealousy anytime they feel the safety and comfort provided by their partner are threatened by another's advances. Alpha's reactions tend to be aggressive toward the potential suitor, whereas the Beta's reaction is likely to be more passive-aggressive. As an example, an Alpha who is threatened may speak directly to the intruding suitor; a threatened Beta would probably talk badly about the intruding suitor to others.

To get beyond feelings of jealousy, you need to understand what's causing you to feel threatened. Is the threat real or imagined? Often we misread innocent actions, such as flirting, as cues of true danger. But if you are uncomfortable, be clear with your partner about those feelings. Don't accuse him of causing a problem; simply say you are feeling uncomfortable. You would hope he will not become defensive and will reassure you that there is nothing wrong.

If there is a reason to worry, meaning your partner is interested in another suitor, understand that he's human. Being interested in others is a natural reaction. Following up on those desires, though, requires a conscious decision.

Whenever there is a chance for either partner to have an encounter outside the relationship, either simply for sex or for the more complex situation of sex with emotional attachment, a decision must be made by the two of you, together. Though many men will insist that this is their decision, and theirs alone, I disagree. Anyone who has agreed to be part of a relationship has an obligation to his partner, especially on a matter that can so strongly affect both of you.

The two of you need to discuss it. If it is your partner who is considering an encounter outside the relationship, either you can allow him to explore his outside interest, within limits that you both feel comfortable with, or he has to forget the whole thing. Period. The bottom line for dealing with jealousy is this: you both are men; at times you both will find other men attractive. Acting or not acting on those desires has to be a joint agreement.

Perhaps the best way to look at potential outside encounters is this: for the partner who is interested in someone outside the partnership, try to understand your partner's fears. If you love him, you won't want him to be frightened or fearful. On the other hand, if your partner tells you he would enjoy an outside experience, you should consider it a potential gift. If you love your partner, and he says this experience would make him happy, perhaps you should consider it.

Of course, one's personal moral and religious beliefs should be considered in these matters.

AVOIDING THE CHEMICAL LOVE LETDOWN

The high we feel when we fall in love with someone has a significant evolutionary purpose: to crank up our attraction to the person, at least long enough for us to successfully reproduce, if we are heterosexual. For gay men, the early part of falling in love is just as euphoric—so much so that when these feelings begin to fade, as they always will after the first two years of a relationship, we find ourselves confused. Are we falling out of love? Not necessarily. Our relationships are just maturing. But for many, these early days become the emotional standard for their future assessment of the relationship, a dangerous idea that can lead many gay men to end a relationship way too soon.

Once you find your true love, you'll be doing it like rabbits. That's because the initial drive in human mating, lust, is facilitated by the production of testosterone. Testosterone stimulates an *indiscriminate* scramble for physical gratification. Lust turns into attraction once a more or less appropriate love/sex object is found. That's your new boyfriend.

This initial rush is, in and of itself, pleasurable, as any man can tell you. The testosterone rush is a natural stimulant to both the body and the brain.

Such testosterone stimulus responses are easily triggered and easily misread by gay men. As Professor Arthur Aron from State University of New York at Stonybrook has shown, in the first few meetings, people often misinterpret certain physical cues and feelings. Notably, fear and thrill—both feelings similar to testosterone rush—may be misinterpreted as falling in love. As such, many gay men may find themselves with mixed feelings, unsure of what is happening in the early stages of dating, as they find they are sexually stimulated by their date but are confused by also feeling competitive with him. If we toss in the fact that a majority of gay men report having some form of anxiety when first dating, and that anxiety is often misunderstood to be sexual stimulation, you begin to see why gay men are more likely than any other group of people to have sex on the first date.

Moving from lusty sex to fulfilling emotional connection requires an increase in the degree of involvement with each other and stimulates the production of a new hormonal chemical, PEA. This is the "falling in love" chemical, designed evolutionarily to assure a period of between two and four years for a couple to mate and for the resulting offspring to survive the first, most dangerous years of life. (The same hormone is stimulated in women during insertive sex, which may be the basis of their desire to cuddle after coitus. Though I have not seen any studies on this, in my clinical practice, I have noted that the anal receptive male partner tends to display a higher level of similar behaviors, such as cuddling, kissing, and emotion, after intercourse. It may be possible that the process of being the receptive partner triggers a heightened level of PEA hormone in gay men as well.)

The production of this hormone begins the emotional cascade that we have grown to know as falling in love. Often, men in the early months of a new affair will have pleasant, yet obsessive, thoughts about their new partner and will see him in a distorted way, overlooking his flaws, flaws that all his friends can easily see.

PEA is also an effective catalyst to heighten the effectiveness of other emotionally positive neurotransmitters: dopamine, adrenaline (norepinephrine), and serotonin. Both partners, again in a stimulus loop, begin to feel giddy. Falling in love is a heady experience. No wonder so many of us become obsessed with it! Nothing can compare to those feelings.

The final stage of bonding in long-term relationships occurs when PEA is replaced by two other hormones (endorphins) known to play a role in social interactions, including long-term bonding: oxytocin and vasopressin. Vasopressin, in particular, has been shown to facilitate monogamous bonding.

So, put simply, the mating system is designed to function in three steps: initial lusty attraction, followed by emotional bonding, and finally, the bond of a contented, lifelong connection. Once a relationship is established, and infatuation has given way to a more stable and less exuberant relationship, levels of testosterone and PEA, as well as the other neurotransmitters, return to "pre-love" levels—a sign of a maturing love.

POWER DIFFERENTIALS

A key concern that every gay couple should be aware of is often overlooked: the use and abuse of power. Power is simply how decisions are made, and who makes them. We usually see two types of problems in an unbalanced power differential.

The first involves the abuse of power, often by the Alpha partner, who feels that his position allows him to be director of his partner's life. Decisions about matters such as money and its allocation, how one is employed, and even home decorating have all sent couples into therapy. The Alpha partner must understand that he holds greater power in certain areas and that his Beta partner has his areas of special knowledge. Additionally, the unique perspective that each partner brings to the relationship, be it spending of money or a knowledge of decorating, generally allows for a balanced look at the issue. In cases of decision making, two heads are better than one, if both opinions are treated equally and respectfully.

The second type of power-related problem involves responsibility. What happens when one partner refuses to take his share of responsibility for decisions within the partnership? All too often I will hear a client say, "Well, *he* was the one who thought that was a good idea." In a healthy relationship, both partners will have input into decisions and accept equal responsibility for their outcome. This allows you to share in successful decisions and helps defuse the impact of poor decisions.

SEX

Contrary to the common belief, many gay couples do run into occasional problems when it comes to sex. Often these problems are temporary, but at other times the problem between the two

"You were terrible sex."

"No, I wasn't, you were."

"I never heard that from anyone before you…"

"You obviously never had good sex before me."

"Whatever. Good now, though. I must have taught
   you…"

"Yeah, that's it. Whatever. But it is really good now,
   that's for sure."

"Wanna do it now?" [They laugh.]

—*Mark and Martin, 60 and 55*

partners may be permanent. A list of sexual dysfunctions and their treatment can be found in many other good books, so I will not cover specific issues here. If sexual dysfunction is a problem in your relationship, I recommend that, as a first step, you speak to your family physician, as the majority of sexual disorders are physically based. He or she is well trained in this area and can provide you with good information.

I feel the greater need concerning sex in this book is the explanation of how the Alpha/Beta dynamic directly affects sex within the relationship. We asked our respondents, "If you could engage in only one type of sexual encounter, what experience would you choose?" and gave them a choice of being the oral active partner (giving a blow job), the oral passive partner (receiving a blow job), mutual oral sex (69), anal passive partner (being on bottom), or anal active partner (being on top). The majority of men, 65 percent, answered that they would choose being the anal passive partner. The second most common answer, 35 percent, was being the anal active partner. These numbers correlated to the number of men who met the Beta male profiles and the Alpha male profiles, respectively, though they were not an exact match.

The evidence is strong that sex role plays a part in healthy relationships as well. This is good news for those relationships that are consistent with the Alpha/Beta dynamic. One problem that arises when the Alpha/Beta dynamic is disregarded is sexual incompatibility. But sexual incompatibility alone is not a basis for ending a relationship.

Surprised? Here's what I mean. No complete long-term relationship is based solely on sex. As relationships age and change, so do their sexual connections. What may have been arousing early in the relationship now may be boring. Other sexual activities may have become arousing. Sex is a skill that is learned. Great sex occurs between men who have a strong emotional bond and a feeling of safety with their partner. So if your sex life isn't staggering right off the bat, or is staggering initially but loses its luster for a while, don't give up.

Early in a relationship, partners are learning how to be with each other, discovering each other's likes and dislikes, finding a sense of comfort and safety. There is, of course, a biological explanation for this. The human body is equipped with a nervous system designed for survival: fight or flight. The system is designed to be both arousing, for running away or fighting, and then calming, to soothe the body after the danger has passed. Interestingly enough, human sexual response is divided between these two systems. Sexual arousal is wired into the fight-or-flight response system, but orgasm can occur only when the environment is safe from danger. Thus, while early in a relationship, sex may be highly focused on arousal, later the sexual relationship moves into a deeply satisfying experience of safe and secure sex. Many men assume that once the arousal focus is gone, the relationship is in trouble, when it is exactly the opposite. Once a sense of security is achieved, you are both safe to explore your deepest sexual selves, including exposing yourselves not only physically but emotionally as well.

As obvious as it may seem, the simple reality of human relations is this: we like people who like us. If you express that like through your sexual expressions as well, generally you'll find yourself in a happy and fulfilling sexual relationship. In happy couples, this becomes a golden circle. By expressing affection for your partner, your partner will increase his expressions of affection for you.

WHAT ABOUT BATBOY?
GAY MEN HAVING CHILDREN

As adoption and surrogacy become increasingly available for gay couples, more and more gay men are choosing to have children. As is true with heterosexual couples, the benefits and costs to a couple and their relationship are many, both good and bad.

In gay couples, the striking thing I have noticed is that when a child becomes a member of a family, the child seems to know intuitively which partner is the Beta and which is the Alpha. It was certainly true in our household. Our son, adopted at the age of twenty months, immediately attached to me as his primary comforter and caretaker, a role I was happy to take on. It was also the role my partner and I had intended. I had the more flexible schedule and was able to take time off to care for our new son while my partner, who also made more money than I did, continued to work (another traditional Alpha/Beta division).

What was more striking was how predictable our behaviors became. For the most part, I was the diaper changer and feeder. My partner, the Alpha in our home, was the roughhouser and disciplinarian. When our son awoke in the night, I was up in a flash, while my partner snored away. I was the one who went to parent-tot classes, while my partner went to work. As our son aged, the pattern continued, in surprising ways. In preschool, without prompting, our son brought home Mother's Day gifts to me and Father's Day gifts to my partner. He even went through a classic Oedipal stage reaction. In a heterosexual family going through the Oedipal stage, the son would reject his father and be drawn to his mother. Often in this stage, a child will say things like "I hate Daddy" and "I want to marry Mommy." In our household, it was "I hate Daddy" and "I want to marry Papa." Go figure.

Gay couples who are well established as a couple will tend to rise to any problems that may come. Gay couples who are not well established may begin to see those cracks grow larger as the pressures of having a child begin to wear on their relationship. Personally, we feel that having a child has made our lives 100 percent better. It's given us a profound sense of time's passage and a greater sense of tradition, and has truly made us feel like a family.

In addition, having a child has opened doors to worlds we never would otherwise have seen. From PTA meetings to neighborhood gatherings, we have become close friends with people we would have never known without a child. The rewards we have received, and the obligations we have taken on, are at times overwhelming, but I would not change a thing for the world. The most common comment I hear from gay men is, "I'm too selfish to have a child." Trust me, that self-focus goes out the window pretty quickly. And you'll be a better man as a result of getting rid of that self-focus. That's not to say that there aren't men and women, gay and straight, who are not cut out for parenthood. Just don't assume because you're gay that you're one of them.

MONOGAMY

A major question for many gay couples is, "Should we be monogamous or have an open relationship?" Though many men may be unhappy with the answer, our research indicates that healthy couples pass from monogamy to an open relationship and then back into monogamy. Perhaps a better question to ask is, "Does monogamy or the lack of monogamy affect the long-term chances for a relationship?" Most research into long-term relationships between men indicates that at some point in a long-term relationship, one, if not both, of the partners will have a sexual encounter outside the primary relationship. Though this isn't a true "open" relationship, it does indicate that the drive for new and different sex partners is strong for almost all men. In a world where sex for gay men is readily available, the more exposure you have to available gay men, the more likely that sex will occur outside the relationship.

I believe that every gay couple must address this question, and that the healthiest choice is to acknowledge that outside sex is likely to occur, and to discuss and agree on what is and isn't acceptable. Of course, for many gay couples, there is a religious or moral concern to sex outside the relationship. For these couples, it is essential that the subject be discussed in detail, and for them to agree that their policy is no outside sex. But even these couples should realize that it still could happen. In fact, there has been some research within the heterosexual community that indicates that the more adamant a partner is about monogamy, the more likely he or she will break that agreement. We try to control in others what we are most afraid of in ourselves. Think of the gay men, generally hidden Alphas, who have taken on public jobs as gay rights opponents, while leading a secret gay sex life themselves.

For other gay couples, the best plan is to preplan for what may come. Though some men may be worried about giving an implied consent, and thus increasing the likelihood of an outside sexual encounter, the opposite is generally true. For many men, sexual adventures outside their relationships are simply a reaction to feeling trapped. Loosening the constraints lowers, but doesn't exclude, the possibility of your partner seeking outside sex. Other guidelines for outside sex can lower the likelihood. A very effective tool is to ask that before any sex occurs, both partners have to be aware of the possibility and agree to allow it to happen.

It is essential that partners understand three key points in order for this to work. First, nature is what drives a desire for outside sex, not a lack of sexual satisfaction at home. Second, you both will have desire for outside sex, but not necessarily for the same person. And third, allowing outside sex should be considered a gift from your partner, not a right—you gave up that "right" when you got into a relationship. If seen as a gift, this allows your partner to have a key power: the veto. When you tell your partner beforehand, he has the right to say yes or no, for whatever reason. No questions asked. If your partner uses the veto, you have to ask yourself, What's more important, my marriage or sex with a stranger?

Of course, all men have the ability to sneak around on their partners. I assume you want a healthy, honest relationship. I have all too often heard men say they keep any outside sexual experiences from their partners in order to "protect them." Trust me, the only thing you're protecting is that poorly constructed house of cards you call a relationship. Outside sex is a minor problem compared to other things that could happen in a relationship. And if one of those problems comes along, you'll need something quite a bit stronger than a lie to stand on.

So, who is more likely to have an affair, Alphas or Betas? It depends on how you define an affair. An Alpha man is more likely to have an emotional affair, which in turn increases the likelihood of damage to his primary relationship. Betas, on the other hand, are more likely to take outside sex less seriously, and have a series of "quickies," often anonymously. While Alpha mates may see these contacts as threatening, they are less likely to result in the Beta mate wanting to leave his primary relationship. Another way to look at it might be this: Alphas prefer emotional dating to physical sex; Betas prefer physical sex to emotional dating, when it comes to affairs.

CHAPTER 14

Mermaid Man and Barnacle Boy in Retirement: The Later-Life Challenges of Individuals and Couples

AS MUCH AS WE MAY WANT to deny it, we all age. From infancy we move into early childhood, then we're transformed via adolescence and feel as if we'll forever live in young adulthood. This is followed by the shock of suffering through a midlife crisis, only to find ourselves in retirement way too soon and looking at the onset of old age. At least, historically, that's how aging was experienced. What was old age for our fathers is now considered later middle age, as we continue to push the limits of aging. A hundred years ago, men tended to live into their fifties, whereas now we can expect to live at least twenty years more, if not longer. As a result, the aging stages of men have shifted.

Gay men, who have historically gone through a slightly different set of developmental stages, primarily a delayed social adolescence, continue to shift these aging expectations as well. Dating is a common feature through all stages of gay life, accompanied by a higher level of sexual activity well into old age.

THE DECLINE OF YOUR SUPERPOWER: TESTOSTERONE

Most life stages are a reflection of the biology that accompanies them. This is certainly true of adolescence, a period when we move both socially and physically from youth to reproductive adulthood, and of menopause, which bridges a woman's life from the reproductive years to late middle age. Though not as well defined as menopause, a similar transition occurs in the life of men. Andropause, a period of time in which testosterone production slowly declines over the middle and later years, results in a lessening of masculine traits. The transition for men from high levels to lower levels of testosterone production is stretched out over decades, the decline becoming most obvious in the forties and continuing into old age. Testosterone production declines approximately 10 percent each decade after males hit their peak levels in their early twenties. Thus, by the time a man turns fifty, he may have lost as much as 40 percent of his testosterone production.

As testosterone is the key chemical translator of secondary male attributes, a decrease in testosterone results in a decrease in outward signs of masculinity both in the body, as seen in a decrease in muscle strength and bulk, and in behavioral traits, such as aggression and libido.

The evolutionary intent of andropause was to decrease aggression in men, so that in these later years they could assist in nurturing the family's offspring. With the decrease of testosterone in older men and the decrease of estrogen in women following menopause, we see older men and women growing to look amazingly similar, as men grow more feminine and women more masculine.

Our two main divisions of gay men go through andropause with marked differences. For gay men who are within the higher levels of androgen expression, Alphas, these changes

You ask if we still have sex. It depends on how you define "sex," I suppose. Do we still "stick it" to each other? No, not really. But we still get naked and enjoy the amazing sensation of skin to skin, the weight of his body against mine, the smell and tastes. But probably the greatest thing for us is kissing. Now our favorite thing to do is simply look into each other's eyes, kiss, and jerk off. We may not be big shooters anymore but let me tell you, the emotion hasn't been any better than it is now.

—*Artie, 80*

over time mirror those of their heterosexual brothers. But those Beta gay men who have naturally lower levels of testosterone expression and fewer androgen receptor sites face significantly greater changes in their lives. In other words, for the more masculine Alpha gay man, changes in old age will be a standard softening of their masculinity, but for Betas, who are already more feminine to start with, the change will be even more significant, as the subtle masculinity they displayed in their younger lives ebbs away.

The result? Beta men, used to depending on their youth and boyish looks to attract mates, face a new problem: how to keep or attract a mate in their later years (just as heterosexual women do, especially after a divorce). In andropause, Beta men's bodies begin to appear more feminine, and feminine behaviors, which have been masked by their youth, also become more noticeable.

Alpha men also show a marked decline in their mateability, primarily because of the decline in testosterone. Youthful Beta partners are highly drawn to the external markers of masculinity, including an upright posture and a confident air, which naturally diminish with age. For those Alpha men who retain their financial well-being, concerns of losing attractiveness are counterbalanced by the Betas' desire for a secure future, something a wealthy Alpha can continue to offer.

The impact of andropause, on both Alpha and Beta men, is a lessening of power. Testosterone plays a role in both mating styles, and with its ongoing decline, being considered *traditionally* attractive declines. For all men seeking a life partner in later life, the challenges are greater, but not impossible. I will note that the majority of men who have been in successful long-term relationships met, and married, earlier in their lives, usually in their late twenties and early thirties.

PROBLEMS FACED BY OLDER SINGLE MEN

For Alpha men who are single at this time of life, the traditional factors they have used to draw a mate, such as masculine facial features, are not going to work now that those traits have been softened by age and lower testosterone. The older Alpha male should focus instead on his essential attractive traits, those traits that have been unaffected by physical changes in appearance. Beta men, no matter what their age, seek men who provide safety, security, and guidance. Highlighting these traits will be to Alpha's advantage as he looks for a mate.

A sad problem arises when Alpha men, even this late in the game, continue to rely on mating skills that "used to work." Many of these men insist on attempting to use their bodies as a tool to attract mates. A great set of pecs does catch the eye of most Betas, but if those pecs are sixty-five years old, the draw is lessened by age, simply because the shape and texture of those muscles has changed. The use of hair dye, hair transplants, facial creams, and youthful clothing all tend to backfire, and instead highlight the very traits the Alpha male is trying to hide. Extremely dark hair on a man with an aged face draws immediate attention to both his wrinkled face and his false hair color, leaving the viewer to think that not only is this man trying to fool him but that he's trying to fool himself as well.

The second problem with most Alpha men in this stage of life is an obsession with youthful partners. This is the Alpha's dilemma: a decreasing masculinity coupled with an increasing desire for youthful partners who are seeking highly masculine men. It is a losing proposal.

What most Alpha men fail to realize at this stage of life is that the Beta trait they are most in need of is not the physical body of youth, but the *nature* of youth. The older Alpha man who seeks a partner who is lively, funny, giving, and joyful will find himself in a more satisfying relationship than if he were with a man half his age. There is an obvious explanation for this. Alpha men have been hard-wired to seek sexually reproductive mates, yet at this stage of life the need for mating sexuality has passed. It is companionship that is needed most at this stage of life, along with companionship sex. Such partners, partners who are "alive with youth," can be easily found in Beta men within ten years of their age. This means that if an Alpha male is sixty-five, a good partner for him would be between fifty-five and sixty-five. The partner's age is less important than his personality.

Just as it is true for heterosexual men, the older Alpha man with money is in a better position to find mates than Alpha men without. Though many find this fact distasteful, the truth is that Beta men are drawn not to money per se, but to the implied safety and security that such money brings. Alpha men providing for their younger Beta male partners have been a standard arrangement for gay couples throughout history.

For Beta men in this age range, problems finding a life partner lie in a similar vein. They are attracted to younger, masculine Alpha men, unconsciously seeking protection from an unsafe world. The heterosexual equivalent would be an older woman with a younger man, something that seems naturally uncomfortable to us. Though such situations do occur, they're pretty rare. The same is true for the gay world. Though many older Beta men may fantasize about being swept up in the arms of some young stud, the reality would be awkward, and unlikely to work. The problem with this arrangement is that Alpha men are naturally drawn to men who are younger than they are, primarily so that their ability to provide and protect is most naturally in place.

For the older Beta man seeking a partner, the key is to recognize the essential masculinity that resides inside the older Alpha body. Find the masculine personality within the Alpha man who is around your age or slightly older.

For both older Betas and Alphas who are seeking a life partner, the key, as has been stated many times before, is to be yourself. Honesty in appearance and behavior is much more attractive to others than surface attraction. The essence of a relationship is not the bodies that attract but the personalities that connect.

For both Beta and Alpha men who are aging, the possibility of hormone replacement therapy should be considered if the symptoms of low testosterone become a problem. Signs of low testosterone include lethargy, mood swings, depression, "brain fog," loss of libido, anger, hot flashes, and anxiety. Testosterone for men is, to a certain degree, the Holy Grail—the essence of masculinity—but it is not the fountain of youth. So, many gay men find themselves drawn to use, and sometimes abuse, anabolic steroids, which are artificially produced copies of human testosterone. I am not a medical doctor, but I do highly recommend you discuss this issue with your doctor if you are tempted to do so. If your doctor feels there's a need for hormone replacement therapy, he or she will prescribe an appropriate amount of testosterone from a reliable source.

PROBLEMS FACED BY AGING COUPLES

The aging Alpha/Beta couple presents a unique set of problems. The decline in testosterone and the sexual familiarity that comes with time together often combines to create boredom for many gay couples in their middle years together. Sexuality for the older couple may be problematic in certain ways, but much more beneficial in other ways. It is important for couples to remain sexually active, as this is probably the best form of communication between partners, conveying love in a way that nothing else can match. Much older gay couples tend to have less active sex, and often engage in sex without an orgasm. Any form of physical contact is highly desirable and beneficial, according to our older respondents, who report having some form of sexual contact on an average of twice a month.

If the couple survives the troubling middle years (Year 5 through Year 10 as a couple, or from age thirty-five to sixty), the chances of being together for life are greatly increased. By the time couples are approaching their later years, most have resolved any issues of power, control, direction, and sexuality. At this point in life, more profound issues come to the forefront for the couple. Each member may question his purpose in life, as well as the purpose of the relationship. In general, though, coupled men report these later years as being some of their best together.

For many men transitioning into their later years, a key problem that has to be addressed is the loss of sexual power, not in the sense of sexual performance ability but of respect within the gay community. As much as we may find it uncomfortable, all too often one's sexual appeal is a key component in how one is treated, especially by younger gay men. For those gay men who have relied heavily on their sexual attractiveness to garner respect from others, the aging process will be most difficult. It is essential to all gay men, both Alphas and Betas, to find other ways to validate their lives. Those men who have a strong sense of accomplishment in their lives tend to report greater support from others around them. Those men who continue to seek validation from others will find their sense of well-being in danger.

Metaphysical questions of "why am I here?" and "what is my purpose in life?" are common for all people in this phase of life. For most women in our society, old age is a time for continued value, as mentor, as grandmother, and as holder of family traditions. Many men find contentment from managing their life's accumulations, both monetary and material goods, as well as passing on the tools of business with a gentle, guiding hand to their sons and daughters.

Many gay men struggle with their purpose late in life because of the lack of children in their lives. For all older men and women, depression has become a national problem. For gay men, it can be even greater. An overwhelming sense of loneliness can lead to major depression.

For aging Beta men, it is essential to find some way of using your essential skill of nurturing for the benefit of others. Many Beta men find providing care and comfort for the sick in our community to be rewarding. Others have taken on the role of holders and executors of family traditions, maintaining contact, communication, and the history of their families. For those men who have severed ties to their families, reconnecting with their siblings and, if still alive, their parents can be helpful at this time in life. I had a client who had not spoken with his father for years, but as he became more aware of his own aging, he wondered how his father had successfully moved from being a highly sexual man (he had been quite the womanizer in his youth) to someone who could find contentment in old age. This first question led to a reconnection, providing for his father the role of guide again and, for my client, a reestablishment of his place in time and family.

For aging Alpha men, the most important role they can play is mentor for young men coming behind them, especially in helping those who are involved in business. Though all gay men have an ethical responsibility to the well-being and advancement of those gay men coming behind them, Alpha gay men, who may have been hidden in the past due to fear of being exposed as being gay, can take on a more public role now that there is little threat to their well-being. Doing so returns these Alpha males to their most comfortable roles: provider and guide.

DEATH, GRIEVING, WIDOWERHOOD

Though I have no direct evidence, I have had multiple cases in my practice where this pattern has played out. As in hetero-sexual couples, I have noticed that it is common for the Alpha member of gay couples to die earlier than the Beta partner. One obvious reason is that Alphas tend to be older than their mates. It could also be that the physiology of Alpha males mirrors that of heterosexual men, who tend to die earlier than women. Beta males who remain after the death of their partners often enter into a form of "widowerhood," in which, like women who have survived their husbands, they find themselves in a new, often unwanted independence. Unlike most elderly women, though, the need for sexual expression for these widowers tends to still need an outlet. As a result, many widowed Betas find themselves in the classic Beta dilemma, searching for a protective and providing masculine male without the youthful sexuality to offer in exchange.

Many men in this situation feel their best recourse is to hire a male escort. Though this does generally meet their physical needs, often their emotional needs become entwined in these encounters, to their detriment. I have seen many widowed Beta men hire an escort, only to fall in love with the young man. Usually these situations don't work out. Beta men who find themselves in these situations have two options: either seek other older men for companionship and perhaps find a suitable new partner, or do as many widows do: start a new, single stage of life, finding joy in your memories.

The death of a partner does not necessarily have to mean the end of the relationship. As partners find support, guidance, and meaning from their relationships even when not physically together, even after death, these functions can continue. In doing so, you continue to benefit from the relationship, and in this way experience a love that does last forever. If your love was essential to your well-being, it will continue to be so, even if you two are separated indefinitely.

All couples, throughout their lives together, need to ask themselves what the purpose of their connection is, what it is that they are trying to create by being together. A couple is, as the saying goes, a sum greater than the value of its parts. What is that sum, *that purpose,* for you and your partner as a couple? This essential question is relevant from the first day you two spend together, and will remain relevant to your very last minute together. And it is this question that will be most obviously answered once one of you is gone. If you know that answer, you will be better prepared to spend your lives together and to celebrate it once one of you is no longer around.

Tomorrow and Beyond

Batman: Who invited you?

Robin: I was just hanging around.

Batman: I thought you were gonna stay in the museum. Round up some thugs.

Robin: How 'bout, "Nice to see ya? Glad you're here to save my life."

—*Batman and Robin, 1997*

RIGHT NOW, a man is heading to a local coffee shop. When he gets there, he'll chat with the barista, buy a paper, and have a seat in the front window. He'll casually scan the others in the shop as he folds the paper in half. No one will realize that he's lonely and looking.

Right now, a man is buying groceries for one. He'll make his way through the store, deciding, time and again, how much he needs to buy, recalculating recipes for one person, aching, just once in his life, to cook dinner for two.

Right now, a man lies awake in the dark of his bedroom, the man he thought he loved sleeping far away, even though he's in bed right next to him. He plans on moving out, afraid but certain there is no hope for his marriage, not realizing that his pain is the same pain of the man sleeping next to him.

Right now, a man sits in a college class, looking at the back of the head of the guy in front of him, noticing how nice his hair is. He imagines what the young man's hair would look like, all messy, falling across his forehead, when he wakes in

Here it is 2005, and I can remember the first time I ever saw his face. It was 1945, sixty years ago. He had just gotten home from the war and had taken a job as a bellboy at a hotel. I worked in a little theater group that put on a revue there. I first saw him coming through the swinging doors of the kitchen. He had a sandwich in one hand—he was always hungry. It was love at first sight.

He asked me to take him on a tour of the hotel, since he was new. I couldn't tell if he was gay or not, but I knew he was definitely cute. He was twenty-five, I was nineteen.

As I showed him around, we found ourselves in the presidential suite and somehow he bumped up against me, I could feel he had a hard-on. I said something smart about being careful with that thing. I was so nervous. He grinned and took my hand and leaned in for a kiss. I guess he could tell I was gay, 'cause he didn't seem hesitant in the least. We ended up doing it right there in the suite.

It wasn't a smooth start, though. He wasn't sure he

the morning. He doesn't realize that the young man sitting in front of him wonders the same thing about him.

Right now, a man laughs at his wife's joke, as they sit elbow to elbow at a small table in a nice restaurant. She's thinking how handsome he is; he's thinking how handsome the waiter is; both are wondering why nothing feels the same anymore.

Right now, in a bookstore, a man is scanning the cover of this book, nonchalantly looking around the store, wondering if anyone has seen him in the gay book section, at the same time hoping the handsome man across the aisle has noticed him, has noticed the two men on the cover of the book, and hoping one of them has the nerve to say "hi."

wanted to settle down. He wasn't even sure he was gay. He went off and dated girls for a while, but always made his way back to my bed eventually. Finally he gave up any pretense of being straight. He told me I "worked his nerve" too much. He told me he just couldn't resist my draw. We moved in together and never looked back. On June 12, 1952, at my insistence, we exchanged rings, privately in our little backyard garden. But it meant a lot to me and, I think, to him. He never took that ring off.

Over the years we faced some tough times, but we were always together. We had our doubts, our affairs, our anger and joy. He grew old. I, of course, didn't. [Smiles.] We adapted to everything that stood in our path. Whatever happened to us, good or bad, was faced together. Together.

[Frank leaned down and softly kissed Joe's face before the attendants closed the coffin.]

—Frank, 80, from a eulogy
he wrote for his partner's funeral

Right now, you hold this book in your hands, having read it, more aware now than ever of how many times a day opportunity passes before you—opportunity to meet someone new, to help someone who is lonely, to meet the man you have always wanted in your life, to strengthen and deepen your relationship.

Right now, you are more aware than ever that way too often you have let these chances pass, allowing those "public performances" that hide our deeper emotional selves to convince you that no one is lonely, no one is looking, no one needs what you have, there is no one you'd ever want, that, basically, there is *no one for you.*

Too often you have allowed this assumption to drive your relationships, assuming that this is the best it can be, assuming the next one will be better, assuming that everyone else's marriages are perfect, just not yours.

Yet right now, you know better. We have gone through this book together, so I know you know better. We have seen how biology plays a role in successful relationships. We have seen what type of mating behaviors you feel most comfortable with. We have seen that no matter what type of guy you are, Alpha or Beta, there is a good match out there for you, for the *true you,* not someone you have pretended to be. We have learned a new way of approaching men, any man, in a way that will create a connection that could well lead to two possible outcomes: a great friendship or a great marriage. We have seen how, regardless of your age, there are always men available for healthy, loving relationships. We have seen how to resolve problems instead of quitting. We have seen how love can flow easily, or through a series of convolutions, depending on how many roadblocks we allow. We have seen how to be in love, forever.

Right now, you are lying in bed or sitting in a chair, it may be late at night or early in the morning, but right now, there is no reason to assume there isn't an answer to your needs for love. If you are single, right now the man of your dreams is sitting somewhere thinking about the day you'll show up. If you are unhappily married, right now there are hundreds of things to do to revive your love, to return the spark. Right now, there are answers waiting to be tried out to rediscover the feelings that once were. If you are happily married, right now, turn and kiss your life partner and tell him, "Thanks." When he asks what that was for, simply say, "Everything."

Right now, regardless of the hour of the day, a heart aches somewhere for what you have to offer. Having read this book, we both know that you now have the superhero skills necessary to fight off loneliness, both yours and others'. I know you can do it, but if you still feel unsure, read this book again. I also know it can be hard to accept that we have been given this special knowledge, these working skills that can relieve both our own pain as well as the pain of another. Yet, like every superhero before us, while none of us has arrogantly asked for these powers, we must realize now that we have them and agree to put our own fears aside and answer the call.

There is one amazing thing about being a superhero that so many newbies fail to realize at first. In the process of saving another from the darkness we all fear most, we find our own salvation, through this act of love.

Right now, okay?

Index